INTRODUCTION

It had originally been my intention of including t
companion book to *Bitton (East) Then & Now*, an
a new book when I unexpectedly obtained a manuscript copy of the history work
carried out in 1958 by the ladies of the local Women's Institute, (See Section 1) As
a result of this good fortune, I have been able to re-design the second Bitton book,
to include all old photographs and include a wider selection, as can be seen in the
recently published, and highly recommended book *Around Bitton*,

As far as this book is concerned, the first part sets out the recent history of Longwell
Green, and West Hanham as compiled, in 1958, by the ladies of the Women's
Institute, and includes copies of the original photographs collected by them. Section
2 shows old photographs from the area, either collected over the years by myself, or
have been taken from other collections, to which extent I am extremely grateful to
Janet and Derek Fisher, Mike Tozer and David Elliott for allowing me to share with
you such excellent additional and interesting views. The final part is a record of one
of Longwell Green's most important and long established industries which sadly is
no longer with us, which was started at the end of the nineteenth century by William
Bence, and which grew to be a well respected business involving a local bus
company and an important coach building firm. The story is illustrated with pictures
from the collections of the above named gentlemen, and also from the Peter Davey
collection, who additionally kindly allowed me to copy and use his highly prized
sample tickets issued by Bence Motor Services Ltd during the 1930's; to all of these
contributors I record my appreciation.

My special thanks go to my wife Doreen for her assistance and encouragement, to
my son Tim for his valued computer skills and time given during the preparation of
the book, and last but not least to our close friends Sheila and Richard Brooks for
reading and correcting the proofs. Although I have endeavoured to minimize any
mistakes made, should any exist then they are unfortunately of my own making for
which I apologize and trust that they will not distract you, the reader, from enjoying
the contents of this book.

October 2001   Ian S. Bishop

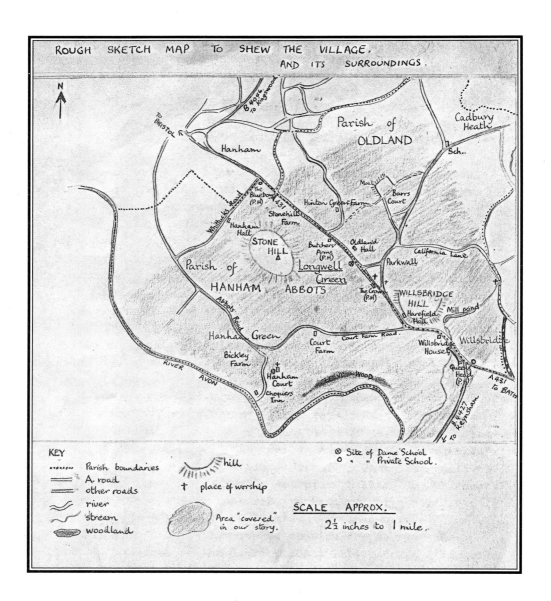

ROUGH SKETCH MAP TO SHEW THE VILLAGE.
AND ITS SURROUNDINGS.

N

To BRISTOL

Hanham

B HOUSE
To KINGSWOOD

Parish of
OLDLAND

Cadbury
Heath

Sch..

Moat

Barrs
Court

The Bluebower
(P.H)

Hinton Great Farm

Whitholds Road

Stonehills
Farm

Hanham
Hall

STONE
HILL

Butchers'
Arms
(P.H)

Oldland
Hall

California Lane

Parkwall

Parish of
HANHAM

Longwell
Green
ABBOTS

The Crow
(P.H)

WILLSBRIDGE
HILL

Harefield
Hall

Mill pond

Abbots Road

Hanham Green

Court Farm Road

Willsbridge

Willsbridge
House

Bickley
Farm

Court
Farm

Queen's
Head
(P.H)

A 431
To BATH

RIVER AVON

Hanham
Court

Chequers
Inn

WOOD

B 4427
To Keynsham

KEY

••••••• Parish boundaries
——— A road
——— other roads
⌇ river
⌇ stream
⬭ woodland

⌢⌢⌢ hill
† place of worship

Area "covered"
in our story.

⊗ Site of Dame School
○ "   " Private School.

SCALE APPROX.

2½ inches to 1 mile.

- 2 -

SECTION 1

THE STORY OF OUR VILLAGE

WITHIN LIVING MEMORY

LONGWELL GREEN, GLOUCESTERSHIRE.

March 1958

ACKNOWLEDGMENTS.

We wish to thank all those who provided us with information and photographs.
We are indebted to the work of the Reverend Canon E. W. Plowright, in his articles written for the Hanham Parish Magazine, and to the following sources :—

Minutes of Hanham Abbots Parish Council;

Minutes of the Management Committee of "All Saints", Longwell Green;

Minutes of Longwell Green Methodist Church and

ELLACOMBE'S HISTORY OF BITTON.

The following history of Longwell was compiled from contributions made by the following members of the Longwell Green Women's Institute, as part of the Gloucestershire Federation of Women's Institute competition entitled "The Story of Our Village"

Mrs.P.Ivens
Mrs.K.Hook
Miss.B.Sambels
Mrs.B.Yuill
Mrs.M.Humphrey

Mrs.P.King
Mrs.M.Finch
Mrs.M.Kemplay
Miss.B.Tugwell
Miss.J.Humphrey

Editors Notes:

Having purchased a manuscript copy of the work carried out in 1958 by the above ladies I felt that the time and effort put into that work was too important to be left unpublished, especially in view of the very obvious fact that Longwell Green has substantially changed and grown over the intervening period and that there were now many new residents who would know little of the history of the village. It was of course possible that the work may have already been published and accordingly it was necessary for me to make enquiries and to clear the way for the production of this book. In doing so I was very fortunate to find and meet two of the above ladies, Mrs Kath. Hook, and Mrs. Pam King, as well as the current President of the Longwell Green Women's Institute Mrs.Beryl Collins MBE. On my behalf they contacted as many of the original ladies as possible and I am extremely grateful to them for giving me permission to allow their work to be published. I am also indebted to Mrs. King and the Committee of the Longwell Green Women's Institute for providing the original photographs.

In preparing their story I have taken the liberty to edit some of their words but the essence of their work remains, as does the period of time in which it was written. I would accordingly remind the reader that the story was written over forty-two years ago and none of the details or time span have been updated.

CONTENTS

* * * * * * * * * *

THE VILLAGE

The village of Longwell Green lies across both sides of the main upper road from Bristol to Bath (The A431) and was until 1842 part of the ancient parish of Bitton, when East Hanham became the parish of Oldland and West Hanham became Hanham Abbots. It derives it's name from one of six common lands in the parish of Bitton known as Westfield, Redfield, Longwell Green, Cadbury Heath, Oldland and North Common all of which were enclosed during the reign of George III by an Act of Parliament of 1819.

The modern spelling of Longwell Green was not officially determined until 1906 when the Bristol Postmaster wrote to enquire the correct spelling, and Hanham Abbots Parish Council settled on Longwell Green and so it has officially remained. Previously in 1813 the Rev. Charles Wayland used the spelling Longways Green in the Baptism Register of Hanham Abbots Church. A year later the Rev. John Pring described the village as Longhurst Green and other reverend gentlemen as Longmans Green, Longhams Green, plus Longwell, Longswells and Longwells Green successively followed. Whilst the latter has continued to be used throughout the first half of this century, it is somewhat surprising that there have been as many spelling variations for a village which has so short a history, however we must bear in mind that a universal standard of spelling did not exist until the latter half of the nineteenth century.

It is a frequently held belief in the original part of the village, commonly termed "The Green" that the name is derived from the existence of a number of springs or wells in the area. The original "long" well is in the front garden of Mr. C Pomeroy's house between the church and the garage. It was bricked up in 1902 and its position was marked on a stone in the wall bordering the footpath. All those who had no well or cistern in their own garden drew water from the long well. There was another well under a path leading up to LONG WELL HOUSE on the opposite side of the road. An account has been given by Mr. H Gully of his father's early morning trek some 80 years ago up the lower slopes of Stonehill via Watery Lane (now Field Lane) to fetch drinking water from a spring near Mount Pleasant farm. Quite often when he arrived, both tired and hot at the spring around 4 or 5 o'clock in the morning, having carried up his wooden yoke and two buckets, he would find two or three other water carriers ahead of him, which would cause him to have to wait for some time before he was able to fill both buckets. His wait could be especially long during the summer months when the spring was little more than a mere trickle, and very often a number of hours would pass before he returned home. At other times when the water was scarce people would go to the top of the hill near Sally on the Barn (this well has only recently been filled in c1957) or to the Goldwell on the hill near Willsbridge House. In Shellards Road, where Mr. H Gully (a builder) still lives there used to be quite a number of cisterns which trapped rain water from the roof tops.

It could be said that the Land Enclosure Act marked the beginning of the true village, as it was at this time during the second decade of the nineteenth century that local landed gentry, Abraham Fry; Robert Nurse (of Hanham Green) and Samuel Budgett, who lived at Oldland Hall, just a stone's throw from the Green, began to enclose parcels of land. Previously there were only a few farm houses and cottages in the area, but gradually the fabric of a village community began to emerge, as more houses were built, leading to the construction in 1856 of the Methodist Schoolroom, followed by the *Crown Inn* in 1861, and the Mission Church in 1896. However the fundamental size of the village did not increase to any great extent until the 1930's, but gained further momentum after the Second World War, when major advances in building and population took place. It is not possible to calculate the number of people living in the village at any given time as it is not a parish in its own right, but is situated on the border-line of the two parishes of Hanham Abbots and Oldland. It is however thought that there were around seven hundred people living in the village during the Second World War, a calculation that is probably made from the number of people requiring gas masks; certainly there are many more people living in the area now.

Coming from Bristol through Hanham, the road descends gradually between green fields stretching to Oldland on the left-hand side, and a long low hill on the right known as Stonehill. From this point there is an excellent view of Kelston Round Tump a group of trees at the top of Kelston hill, which is a landmark for miles around. It is at the area known as Stonehill that the village begins, as it stretches for nearly a mile to the top of Willsbridge Hill, having grown from the few buildings erected on or near the Green during the latter half of the nineteenth century. In the middle of the village, on the opposite side of the original "Green" not to be confused with the conventional village green are the most important buildings, being the Church and Hall; the Methodist Chapel and Schoolroom; the Post Office and General Stores; the garage; the village Inn; the YMCA hut (which mainly serves as the headquarters of the Longwell Green Memorial Association); the grocer, butcher, and draper shops, and the local cafe. In addition there are private houses on both sides of the road, as far as Willsbridge in one direction, and to the Longwell Green Coachworks (now the only local industry) in the opposite direction. The area known, as Parkwall is now an over-spill housing estate built by the Warmley Rural District Council in co-operation with the Bristol City Council for people from the heavily bombed Barton Hill/Easton areas of Bristol. Those who have moved out into the countryside now live, where just five years ago, there was nothing other than country lanes and meadow fields, hedged with blackthorn, bramble and elder and crisscrossed with well defined foot-paths, intermingled with fallow fields and the occasional field of ripening corn. In the near distance small grassy knolls of coal slag were all that remained of the once thriving California Colliery, which had been closed in 1904, by flooding.

At the brow of Willsbridge Hill there is a turning, previously known as Stouts Hill, which leads to Court Farm Road, and to Court Farm itself. At the farm the narrow road bears right, down a short hill before turning left and on to Hanham Court

Church, the hamlet of Hanham Green, and Hanham Court, which is historically connected with Longwell Green by the association of the Creswick family who once lived there, and the Newtons of Barrs Court. In 1910 there were only two or three houses in Court Farm Road, then known as Limekiln Lane due to there being two lime works, one near Albert Villa, and the other near Court Farm at the other end of the lane. There was a cottage halfway along the lane, with another one converted from stables of the upper lime works near Court Farm.

During the first decade of the twentieth century, Mrs.E.Jefferies of Harefield Hall had Field House built where, for some time lived Ernest Swaish the painter, whose picture entitled "The Dawn" was reputed to have sold for one thousand guineas. (£1,100). His studio can be seen from the main Bath Road, but is now used for more utilitarian purposes because Field House is now a poultry farm.

Today, the main road is completely built up except for a corner of what was once the market garden, which extended from the top of Court Farm Road, across the hill, and down one side of it to Bath Road at Longwell Green. On this site, which was sold some two or three years ago, a private housing estate is being built. From Court Farm Road, it is possible to view Bristol to the northwest, the Somerset hills to the west, and the southern end of the Cotswolds at Lansdown. The main road from Longwell Green leads down Willsbridge Hill past Oldbury Chase and the Willsbridge Milling Co., with a glimpse of the millpond on the left, and Willsbridge House on the right. At the bottom of the hill is the *Queens Head*, an inn, which is marked on an old map of about 1670, drawn for Francis Creswick of Hanham Court. Just beyond the inn, the road crosses the Mill Clack or Warmley brook, which flows on until it reaches the River Avon near Londonderry Farm. Having crossed the stream, the road climbs Brockham Hill, on through upper Willsbridge, and then continues along the old Roman Way, through Bitton, Kelston and on to Bath. There stands at the top of Brockham Hill the old turnpike house, now an off licence known as the *Railway Inn*, where the road splits with the right-hand section leading to Keynsham, and the water meadows, having first passed the interesting Londonderry Farm House, with some of its windows blocked up and painted in to look like windows and to save the owners money during the reign of George III, having to pay excessive "window tax" and, on the left Roseneath, once the home of a member of the Creswick family. The Mill Clack brook marks the boundary between the parishes of Hanham Abbots and Bitton.

GEOLOGY

Longwell Green is situated, geologically speaking, in what was known in the nineteenth century as the coal basin of Gloucestershire and Somersetshire. The village, then part of the parish of Bitton, was on the fringe of the Kingswood coalfield, and there was a pit only half a mile away near Oldland. It was known as the California Pit, and was closed in the early years of this century. The workings in the pit were known to stretch as far as the market garden near the main road, with Longwell Green being in the south-east corner of the Gloucestershire area of the

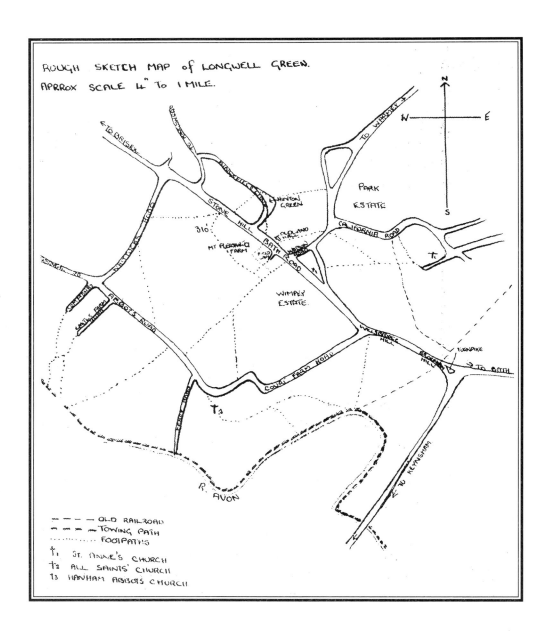

ROUGH SKETCH MAP of LONGWELL GREEN.
APRROX SCALE 4" TO 1 MILE.

N
W ——+—— E
S

← TO BRISEX
PARK ESTATE
TO WICKET
HINTON GREEN
STONE HILL
310
MT PLEASANT FARM
CLELAND MILL
CALIFORNIA ROAD
BATH ROAD
WIMPEY ESTATE
WILLS CROSS HILL
TURNPIKE
→ TO BATH
ABBOTS ROAD
CASTLE FARM
COURT FARM ROAD
T₂
R. AVON
↗ TO KEYNSHAM

— — — OLD RAILROAD
— — — TOWING PATH
·········· FOOTPATHS
T₁ ST. ANNE'S CHURCH
T₂ ALL SAINTS' CHURCH
T₃ HANHAM ABBOTS CHURCH

- 10 -

Above: Looking along the Main Road towards Hanham around 1908 showing the growth of the 'Coronation Trees', with the tin church behind. Below: Today's (1958) view of the same road but this time in the direction of Bitton, showing All Saints' church and hall.

coal basin, the River Avon being the dividing line between the two areas Stonehill Farm, Hinton Green and Barrs Court are all on the fringe of the coal measure.

The river flows between banks of Alluvium, but between the confluence of the Mill Clack stream and Hanham Mills the ground rises steeply through Cleeve Woods, where there are outcroppings of limestone, with beds of lower lias beneath Westfield. The top of Stonehill is also made up of lower lias but additionally includes a small area of inferior oolite.

Most of the village, including the Green, is on new red sandstone, which covers an area stretching roughly from Watson Road, to the bottom of Willsbridge Hill, across in a westerly direction to Hanham Green where it separates, with one section joining the Cleeves near the river, whilst the other section hinges in a north westerly direction to include the lower slopes of Stonehill. Pennant Stone was once quarried in Hanham Woods, just beyond Hanham Mills, and close to the river, and was frequently used in the construction of many of the local houses. With reddish marks in the greyish blue stone, the material has an easily recognizable and very pleasant appearance, particularly when the colours are picked out in the bright sunlight. A slightly unusual local industry, which used to operate at Hanham Green in the eighteenth century, was the manufacture of pennant stone coffins.

FLORA AND FAUNA

From the previous account given of the geology of the district, and the description of the area immediately surrounding Longwell Green, it can be seen that there is a basis of a mixed habitat for both plant and animal life, which consists of woodland; river; water meadows; streams; wooded slopes; quarries and limestone country. The village itself is made pleasant by the number of trees which grow in and around it, small elms in the hedges of surrounding fields, lime trees near the corn mill at Willsbridge, and on the green at Hanham Green, copper beeches and conifers in the grounds of Harefield Hall, with a solitary horse chestnut behind the building. Additionally, there are the beech trees at the entrance to Oldbury Chase, and of course there is the single row of plane trees, which border the roadside for a quarter of a mile from Watson Road, southeastwards through the village.

Willow; oak; hazel and hawthorn can be found in Catscliffe coombe, with many more bordering the stream between the millpond and Oldland Bottom, below St.Annes church. Further afield in the Cleeves, which slope down to the river, are yew trees, whilst a larch grows outside the high wall of Willsbridge House, with another known to be growing in 'the wilderness' which surrounds the old lime quarries in Court Farm Road.

The following is a list of trees which are presently to be found in the parish of Hanham Abbots which, of course, includes part of the village of Longwell Green: oak; elm; ash; birch; beech; alder; hornbeam; hazel; witch elm; maple; sycamore; white, black, and lombardy poplar; willow; yew; scotch pine; holly; spindle; buckthorn; wild apple; mountain ash; hawthorn; dogwood; wayfaring tree; horse chestnut; bay; laburnum; locust tree; larch and walnut. In addition the following flowers have also been found in recent years in the parish: agrimony; arum; anemone; blackberry; bladder campian; bluebells; brook lime; bugle; burdock; buttercup; red and white campian; honey; crimson and white clover; field and great hedge convolvulus; cow parsley; crane bill; cuckoo flower; daisy; ox eye; dandelion; dead nettle; flax; forget-me-not; foxglove; furze, groundsel; hawkweed; heath; herb robert; honeysuckle; wild hop; horehound; yellow iris; mallow; mare's tail; meadowsweet; mustard; pimpernel; poppy; primrose; ragged robin; field rose; shepherd's purse; strawberry; teazel; thistle; vetch; violets; wild carrot, and wood sorrel. The Star of Bethlehem has also been found in Hanham Woods, an indication of limestone country.

A local amateur naturalist has made a keen study of the flora and fauna of Hanham and Hanham Abbots during the last twenty years, and affirms that the animal population of the area is almost static. His records show that he has himself seen during the time of his studies the following animals: –

Reptiles: common lizard; slowworm; the adder or viper; the common grass or ringed snake.

Amphibians: frogs; toads; and crested smooth and palmate newts.

Mammalian: bats; hedgehog; mole; shrew; fox; stoat; weasel. A badger has been reported to have been in the district at various times. Rats; voles; rabbits and grey squirrels, with the latter occasionally seen in the gardens of houses in Shellards Road.

Birds: include mistle and song thrush; blackbird; wheatear; robin; nightingale; black cap; whitethroat; garden warbler; wren; chiffchaff; willow and wood warblers; hedge sparrow; long tailed titmouse; great, marsh, coal, and blue tits; nuthatch pied wagtail; grey yellow and white wagtails; meadow pipit; spotted fly catcher; swallow; house martin; sand martin; goldfinch; house sparrow; chaffinch; linnet; bullfinch; yellow bunting; starling; tawny owl; buzzard; sparrow hawk; kestrel, and heron. In addition there have also been the occasional but rare sight of: cormorant; mute swan; widgeon; wild duck; common teal; tufted duck; ring dove; stock dove; turtle dove; moorhen; coot; golden plover (viewed in flight), lapwing; woodcock; common snipe; curlew; common tern; herring, common, and black headed gulls.

The amateur ornithologist contends that the number of waterfowl has been steadily increasing since the Second World War, and thinks that this may be due to the flooding of Chew Stoke Valley for a reservoir during the last three years, also the establishment of the Wild Fowl Trust at Slimbridge. Of the resident birds, the nightingales in Hanham Woods must be mentioned, an area which is reported to be a good district for these songsters. The number of hedge sparrows is increasing, but the corncrake, heard in the district fifty years ago, is no longer to be found.

BUILDINGS

There are many stone built houses in the village, which are quite interesting, although not of architectural significance. One or two are converted farmhouses, which at one time were refronted as for instance, Oldland Hall. At the top of Willsbridge Hill stands Harefield Hall, which was built, for Mrs.E. Jefferies, in the early 1900's. It is a solidly built grey stone house, with very pleasant grounds, which slopes gently to the road. A few yards further down the hill is Oldbury Chase, built around 1910, and originally called 'Goldwell' after the nearby spring found between the house and the road. Oldbury Chase is considered by local builders to be the finest house in the village due to the splendid quality of the timber and other materials used in its construction. The first person to live there was Mr.F.G.Swaish, who was the Lord Mayor of Bristol during the First World War.

On the other side of the road, opposite the mill and mill pond, is Willsbridge House commonly referred to as 'The Castle' by reason of the mock battlements which were added during 1848 by the then owner of the property Captain Stratton. The house had been built, by an ancestor of R.L.Pearsall, the madrigal writer, who had come to Willsbridge in the early eighteenth century. He lived for many years in an old thatched house by the brook (there is no trace of it now) and towards the end of his life had Willsbridge House built. Originally, it was quite small, being little more than a house extension to a cottage already standing there. The house was further enlarged and completed by his son, whilst his grandson, around 1802, added a coach house and stables.

It is thought that the son of the first John Pearsall constructed 'The Limes' an old house near the Mill, possibly once Oldland Manor or certainly built on the site of the manor, opposite Willsbridge House, and most of the cottages built in that area, but not those adjoining the *Queen's Head,* were constructed by the son of the first John Pearsall.

There is no manor house in Longwell Green, as the one at Willsbridge, which is thought to have been the ancient manor house of Oldland, preceded the construction of the Pearsall properties. The other claimed manor house of Oldland, as described in Ellacombe's "History of Bitton," was Hanham Hall, built around 1655. Hanham Court was of course the manor house of West Hanham. The other large property of note is Barrs Court built on the edge of Longwell Green on land which was once part of the great forest of Kingswood. The now dilapidated court is approached by three

Mill and Mill Pond, Willsbridge.

Two different views of Willsbridge Mill, and Millpond both probably taken around
1905~1910.

MILL POND
WILLSBRIDGE.

long drives from different directions, and is set well back from the road. No one lives there now but the land is farmed by Mr. Hooper from Longwell Green, and quite frequently a tractor and/or cattle truck, looking somewhat incongruous and out of place, is seen on the land. Unfortunately the building is now going to rack and ruin, with roofs and ceilings falling in, whilst creepers form a curtain of foliage over the remaining standing walls which, from a distance, mask the neglect, and hints at what a beautiful building it must have been.

That which remains is only a fraction of the whole manor house itself, and may represent little more than what was once the servants quarters. Even the very large adjacent farmhouse has fallen into disrepair over the past fifteen years. Interestingly there is a room with barred windows within the farmhouse, but whether it was to keep prisoners in, or to keep the farm valuables safe has not yet been determined. Nearby the large dairy has a spring, which runs through it, and some fifteen years ago there was extant a beautiful coat of arms, which has now sadly disappeared, and may well be lost forever.

It is easy to imagine, when visiting Barrs Court, that time has slipped back to say 1483 when Sir John Barr owned not only the house but also much of the land and property for miles around. It was of course from this knight that the property obtained its name but having on his death no surviving male issue to carry on the family name, the property passed to another section of the Newton family, and then to separate Newtons over a number of centuries. One of the early branches of the family were close relations of Sir Isaac Newton of gravity fame, but there is no record that this man of science actually ever visited the Court. In 1540, Barrs Court was described by John Leyland as a *"fayre old manor place of stone, the forest of Kingswood cummys just on to Barrs Court."* The court probably entered its heyday during the 1650's, when Sir John Newton, with the help of the right intermarriages, owned several of the nearby manors as well as Barrs Court. Sir John, who lived for 71 years until 1699 was very prolific having fathered, during his fifty-five years of marriage, no less than four sons and thirteen daughters. His extremely healthy wife out-lived him and, for the seventeenth century reached the magnificent age of eighty-five. Both the fertile knight and his lady, together with a number of their children are buried at St Mary's Bitton, where the following epitaph can be seen: -

"A most loving husband, careful father, faithful friend, pious, just, prudent, charitable, salient, and beloved of all. He was three times burgess of Parliament. Born 1626. Died 1699"

There are other tombs and monuments in respect of the Newtons at Yatton, East Harptree (their ancestral home), and in Bristol Cathedral.

During the early part of the eighteenth century, the court passed into the hands of Sir Michael Newton who married from Herefordshire, Margaret, Countess of Coningsby. Tragedy unfortunately struck this family when, their only infant son was fatally dropped by his nurse as she was descending the stone stairway, having been suddenly confronted by the image of an ape. What caused this image to manifest itself was never determined, as there are certainly no records of the Newtons having ever kept an ape at Barrs Court. There were no other children born to this marriage, and on the death of Sir. Michael the property passed to his widow. When she died in 1746, much of the house was destroyed, possibly due to the fact that there being no heirs, a clause in the Will decreed that the house should be razed.

As the eighteenth century was drawing to an end the following description of Barrs Court was recorded: –

"It was an old house, marked by a moat, with a high wall all round the park. Niches were filled with colossus leaden statutes. The hall was large and lofty, and richly carved. There was gilt all round the fireplace, and a shelf supported by two figures. It was paved with black and white marble squares, complete with a musician's gallery, and a chapel. It had square mullioned windows, and there was a drawbridge. There was a porter's lodge, and a large and a small gateway."

There is at the British Museum a twenty-five foot long parchment which contains a list of Barrs Court tenants, one of whom was the Abbot of Keynsham. Reapers received twopence per day, and there is mention of Monday lands, when the tenant was obliged to work, without reward, for his landlord each Monday. In addition there is another manuscript which belongs to the Newtons of Barrs Court, containing a record of rents paid by tenants from 1729 to 1740, although there are several blank pages after it came into the hands of Thomas Long, a Bristol haulier who used it as a log book.

So Barrs Court has gone on, getting smaller and more dilapidated, but even so, it still has an atmosphere of a great house.

* * * * * * * * *

HANHAM ABBOTS

This village lies about a mile south of Kingswood, with which it is now connected by an unbroken succession of houses. The village was first mentioned during Roman times, when the Via Julia, which ran from Sea Mills to Bath passed through Hanham. Some Roman coffins have been found in Hanham, and a Roman well was recently discovered in the grounds of Hanham Court. The first direct evidence of the existence of Hanham as a place of habitation comes from its name, which is almost certainly one that had been given by the Saxons. The 'Ham' endings which occur in so many place names is a Saxon word meaning home, and the Oxford Dictionary of Place Names states that the name Hanham means either: –

> Hana a cock, or
> Hana a personal name,
> Han a stone

The existence of such places as Cock Road and Cockshot Hill makes it more than likely that Hanham means "the home of the woodcock" a wild bird, which once abounded in the forest.

From very early times, Hanham was divided into two parts, East and West, with the latter becoming more frequently known as Hanham Abbots. The Domesday Book (1086) gives the description of Hanham as Lands of Ernulf de Hisding in the Hundred of Swineshead. Ernulf was succeeded by his son Robert, and afterwards by Marisco of Saltmarsh, the Hanham family having moved to Cheddar. The Manor was sold in the 1320's to William de la Green, and John Bagworth who, in 1330 gave the whole estate to Keynsham Abbey, in whose ownership it remained until the Dissolution of the Abbey around 1525.

The church at Hanham Abbots was built by the Monks of' the Abbey during the middle of the fifteenth century, and it is believed that when a new font was made for the monastery, the monks took the old redundant Norman Font to the new church, together with the Norman Piscina. On the Court side of the church there can still be seen a narrow doorway which has been walled-up, and it is believed that the priest entered the Lady Chapel through this door.

Sally on the Barn.

Limekiln Lane in its rural setting turns sharply to the right as it avoids running through the Court Farm barn known locally as 'Sally on th Barn' c1903

Lime Trees on Hanham Green 1903

The age of the church meant that it was in constant need of repair, and there is no indication within the accounts that any money was ever granted for that purpose by the Mother Church. During 1812, the repair cost was £150, and these were only of a temporary nature as the fabric of the building was rapidly falling into decay. An appeal was made shortly thereafter with the legend: –

"This ancient Church has been lately surveyed and found to be in a very dilapidated state, and the timbers of the roof so decayed, and the walls so forced out of perpendicular and cracked, that the whole fabric is in considerable danger of falling, and no longer safe for Divine Service"

The vestry committee reported that they had voted in a rate amounting to about £150 to be raised towards the estimated expenses attendant upon the necessary repairs to rebuild part of the walls and buttresses, and an almost wholly new roof. However they added a condition which was that the rate would not be charged unless voluntary contributions be collected to remove the present inconvenient pews and have them rearranged so that the sitting afforded better accommodation, and to render the church both lighter and drier by making improvements to the windows and the drainage, all at an estimated cost of £634.4.0 (£634.20p)

It was not until 1854 that the work was completed, and the church re-opened on the 18 October of that year. Since then, further restoration has taken place on two other occasions, the last time being in 1946.

In 1844 the third chapter in the history of St.George Hanham began when it obtained its full independence from the Parish Church of Bitton, becoming in that year a separate ecclesiastical district and elevated to a Mother Church itself following the consecration of Christ Church Hanham in 1842 which then became a Chapel of Ease. This situation lasted for just over sixty years, when in 1905 the position was reversed Christ Church becoming the dominant church of the parish, whilst St. Georges Chapel reverted to the position it knew best.

Throughout its existence, both baptisms and marriages have taken place in this little church, but there has never been a churchyard or burial ground.

Next to the church with its shared south wall stands Hanham Court, a building of great historical age, but exactly when the first manor house was built is not known. What is certain is that a manor house existed before the Conquest in 1066, but whether or not it was on the same site cannot be determined. In 1330 it was conveyed to the Abbot of Keynsham, and no doubt the monks would have enhanced the house and grounds and together with the Abbot, they would have lived a peaceful life there until the Dissolution of the Monasteries. With their power taken from them by Henry VIII, and their properties surrendered to the Crown, the incumbents were less than happy, and it is said that John, the last Abbot to reside at Hanham was so angry at his loss of comfort that he unchristianly laid a solemn curse upon the house.

Some hundred years later in 1638, the Creswick family came to Hanham Court in the form of Sir Henry, a Bristol merchant, who had been knighted by Charles II fifteen years previously, and .who in 1660 became Mayor of Bristol. Despite a high level of emnity between the Creswicks and their near neighbours the Newtons, Hanham Court remained occupied by them for two hundred years until the last of the Creswicks moved out in 1842 From then it ultimately passed by purchase to Major Philip Carlyon-Britton JP, who owned the Court until 1920 when, with the following description it was listed to be auctioned at Hanover Square, London:

RESIDENTIAL PROPERTY of 40 acres. Tudor style residence (13 bed and dressing rooms); garage; stabling; lodge; farmery; pleasure grounds and well timbered park; woodlands; shooting; fishing; hunting, and golf. Situated in the Parish of Hanham Abbots in the County of Gloucester, is a picturesque old residence, standing in a quiet well-sheltered position. It is substantially built in the Tudor style, mostly of stone, with mullioned windows, and is covered with ivy.

As the above already indicates, there are very pleasing surroundings to Hanham Court, with lime trees making a fine avenue on the west side. There were originally four fishponds but only the largest to the north is now apparent. In 1431, during the reign of Henry 11 a survey of the area took place, and recorded that there is a manor house built with proper offices and with ponds, moats and an orchard called 'great orchard' with a barton and a dove cote, which is worth by the year to let to farm twenty shillings. There was at the time a tenant identified as Richard who held eight acres of land for which he paid a half annual fee each Easter of one pair of gloves, or one penny, followed at the feast of St.Michaelmas by half a pound of cummin, or three halfpence.

There are various styles of architecture, with the oldest portion apparently being the west wing with tower, which appears to date back to the Elizabethan times. This aspect of the house, both inside and out have been handsomely constructed, with a stately tower, hexagonal square windows, and has an hexagonal roof with several weird gargoyles, with grinning faces.

The entrance to the Court is through a gateway on the north side, which leads into a Courtyard. There is a very old but sound porch door through which the great Hall lies on the right and contains a fine Tudor fireplace and Tudor doorway, the latter of which is in the north sidewall. There is a modern screen erected in 1850 with a grand staircase on the left of the main entrance. However, although erected in 1630, this is not the original staircase. The small sitting room is on the right and it is believed that this was previously a Library and before being put to that use it was a Justice room. Originally there was an entrance from this small room, which led directly into the Church.

Other features of interest in this house are said to be the peephole on the left of the archway which gives a view of all who enter; a graceful oriel window on the north side; a small square window which faces west and which gives light to what is

The Old barn at Hanham Court c1910

The River Avon at Hanham with the *Old Chequers Inn* c1908.

thought to have once been the gunpowder room and the wonderful old kitchens with their massive arches and low roofs. Additionally, there is the rare Norman barn on the north side, which is a fine architectural building with buttressed walls and a tower.

* * * * * * * * *

Looking up to Willsbridge House 1957

Harefield Hall from Court Farm Road c1955

Sally on the Barn and Court Farm Road 1957

One of the first motorbuses to be operated by Bristol Tramway & Carriage Co on its Hanham Longwells (sic) Green Willsbridge Bitton & Kelston Route. This posed picture has been take in Hanham High Street just past the junction with Victoria Road c.1925.

HANHAM MILLS

If you take a walk across the fields from Longwell Green, down the hill pass Hanham Court with its little fifteenth century Church you will arrive at a delightful stretch of the river Avon known as Hanham Mills. As you look around, it will seem as though time itself has stood still, with the half a dozen or so cottages and the mill house huddled together looking very similar to when they were originally built in 1725. The mill itself is long since gone but it is still possible to see the arches, millrace and foundations where once the mill stood. Nearby, there is an ancient well from which plenty of water was drawn and as recently as only ten years ago, this was the only source of fresh water supply for the cottages. This particular well is by popular legend a Roman construction and it is claimed to have the unique feature that in times of drought or plenty its water level never alters. Of a more recent period prior to the last war, there are many stories of local folk filling buckets, pails, jugs and tin baths with water from this well in order to provide teas for the many thirsty visitors strolling along the river bank.

It is understood that fishing in this part of the river is a delight with plenty of course fish being caught, plus tales being told of trout having been fished from the river in years gone by.

Behind the cottages are the remains of a stone quarry, (owned by Charles. and George Bruton) where in days gone by, stone was taken by horse-drawn carts to river barges for onward carriage to Bristol or Bath and it is understood that the foundations of a number of famous roads within those cities are made from stone quarried at Hanham Mills

This is an extremely picturesque spot within the area covered by this book which we hope will not be spoiled in the future.

* * * * * * * * *

FARMING, MARKET GARDENING & INDUSTRIES.

One hundred years or so ago, Longwell Green was a very different place from that seen today, consisting as it did of a few miners' cottages, which straggled either side of the main Bath Road. In the late eighteenth century the main source of income was derived from agriculture and mining, with the latter becoming virtually extinct about the middle of the nineteenth century, although with the re-opening of the California pit in the late 1880's there was a small revival of mining which lasted for just under twenty years before the pit was flooded out, water being a major problem for all of the coal pits in the Kingswood area.

With the mines closed, the major employers of the relatively cheap labour in the area became farmers and market gardeners, although the more skilled very often worked in the boot and shoe industry. With a productive soil, the main crops were wheat and grass, with apple orchards, dairy and poultry farms dispersed in between. A number of years ago, during the previous century, it is claimed that a man who worked on Parkwall Farm, which belonged to the Barrs Court Estate, was the first in the country to demonstrate the use of a horse-drawn mowing machine. Obviously before such machines were invented, both hay and corn crops were entirely cut by hand using the scythe and sickle. A story is linked with this farmer and his demonstration, which has the Luddite overtones of the 1811-16 period when someone tried to introduce machinery at the feared expense of lost jobs. Progress can be a very difficult matter to come to terms with especially when it appears to directly threaten your job, and ability to earn a living, which in turn threatens the probable well being of your family. Certainly if the story is true then obviously that fear and concern occurred on Parkwall Farm. Apparently, on the day following the demonstration of the new fangled horse-drawn mowing machine, the farmer found two or three of his cow's dead, and this situation was unfortunately repeated over the coming days. Totally baffled by this unusual calamity, and highly suspicious that it was not just a series of unfortunate accidents, he cut open one of the dead cows and found that it had eaten an apple which has been cut in half and stuffed with a mysterious grey substance, which he then arranged to have analysed. A powerful poison was discovered fulfilling the farmer's fears, and although he let it be known that he had discovered the cause of the animals death, and although the poisoning stopped, the culprit was never found, even though it almost certainly had to be one of the farmhands who worked for him. One wonders what that farmer and his employee would make of today's farms where the horse has given way to powerful motor tractors which can be used not only to cut the grass, but with the aid of additional implements can turn the cut grass under the warmth of the sun, and then pick up the hay and throw it out at the other end in a tight bale neatly tied with string. No more hay to cut with a scythe, to turn with a fork, to pitch onto a cart and subsequently to stack and make into a hayrick. Despite all of the obvious improvements, which have been introduced to the farms over the intervening years, many things have been lost to us in the countryside, including some of the charm and picturesque nature of our romantic emotions.

Court Farm, which is situated at the top of what was once Limekiln Lane (Now Court Farm Road), has a very ancient tithe barn, which contains, in the centre pinnacle of the roof, the figure of Ceres, the goddess of corn. More frequently referred to as 'Sally on the Barn', the figure is around six feet tall, and is a well known landmark throughout the district. Another feature of this mixed farm of wheat and pasture is that all of the gateposts are made of stone with each one weighing roughly one ton. The old colloquial name of this farm is 'The Farm on Angels' Hill', and whilst there is no positive proof, it is probable that the figure on the barn helped to create this nickname.

Between 1905 and 1914, the average price of milk at the farm was 6½d (0.2½p) per gallon (4.546 ltrs.) during the summer and 8d (0.3½p) in winter. For many years milk was produced locally by Mr Pearsall, and sold by him throughout the village. Milk was also produced at Londonderry Farm, and became well known in the county for the quality of its Friesian herd, whilst other local farms favoured the Hereford and/or Devon breeds of cattle.

Those who were involved with growing wheat found that in 1906 they were only being paid fourteen shillings for a 140lbs (65½ kilogram) sack. Although the price hardly improved over the next few years, at the outbreak of the First World War, much of the pastureland in the area was ploughed and turned over to the growing of cereals.

It is believed that around 1786 on a plot of about two acres, a market garden was started on the Hanham Abbots side of Longwell Green. The supply of fruit and vegetables to a growing local population and the ever-hungry cities nearby proved to be a success so that by 1917 the market garden had grown to an area covering ninety-seven acres. At the turn of the century, the owner Jason Billing & Sons were producing all kinds of seasonal vegetables and fruit most of which was now despatched to the expanding City of Bristol. Early morning starts at two or three in the morning were a necessity to drive the six miles to the Market, and it was lucky if the carter arrived back in Longwell Green much before mid-day.

Another market garden was set-up just after the end of hostilities in 1918 with the construction during the following year of two new villas in which lived a market gardener who specialized in the growing of chrysanthemums. The soil in this area is reputed to be some of the finest in the West Country for producing quality blooms. With his efforts rewarded, his business prospered and grew and grew, and as he made more money he re-invested it back into the market garden with the construction of more and more glasshouses. He also decided to diversify his cropping by growing very fine tomatoes, cucumbers, early lettuce, and could always be relied upon to have an unsurpassable crop of strawberries in the early summer. Nearly his entire product was sent to the Bristol Market by one of the local carriers

Other notable farms in the neighbourhood are Stonehill, occupied by William

Kyneston in the 1930/40's, and Hinton Green, occupied around the same time by Alex G.Hannam, both farms being part of the Hanham Hall estate owned by the Whittuck's family. In addition there is Park Farm, which has been sold and is now used as a depot for agricultural implements.

From the early days of farming when so much work had to be done by hand, the horse has always played an important part, particularly after the invention of the horse collar which enabled that animal for the first time, to out perform the oxen in hauling heavy loads. Every horse required its hooves to be protected by metal shoes, fashioned by the local farrier who more often than not doubled up as the local blacksmith. Like many villages, Longwell Green had its own family of father to son farriers who worked their busy forge right beside the main road for the convenience of both the traveller and the farmer.

Back in the 1880's the man in charge was George Weston, followed by Arthur Weston who was still classified as the village blacksmith as late as 1939. but it is believed that he may have closed the old forge in the mid 1920's when the use of the horse as a beast of burden gradually began to be superseded by the mechanical tractor and lorry. With the level of blacksmith work also falling the amount of work available was insufficient to sustain a living, and both the farrier and his forge are no more, swept away in the onward march of progress, and in the case of the latter to make a wider pathway.

The active days of the limekilns in the district came to an end in the early 1900's, although it is understood that William H.Worswick continued to earn a living as a lime burner until around 1914. Some quarrying went on to just before the First World War, but business was bad with a rock bottom price of lime down to eight shillings (0.40p) per ton ex works. The machinery for working the quarries was either sold or left to rot, and by the time that the men had returned from the Front the land and buildings had become derelict. With no demand for the local limestone, the land previously used by the quarry owners was gradually put up for sale and sold as building land, and over the years houses have sprung up so that by now (1958) there is hardly a spare plot of land to be had.

At the Bristol end of the village there was at the turn of the century a wheelwright's shop which, after the First World War began to expand by developing a coach building section specializing in building tailor made lorry and bus bodies onto chassis supplied by their customers. Owned by the Bence family, the business grew, and the one time wheelwright's shop has developed into a fair size coach works, spread over a number of acres.

The remaining local farms still produce much the same as they did one hundred years ago, namely milk and grass, but nowadays instead of milking being carried out to the clink of milk pails, and the scraping of mill stools, there is just the hum of the motors driving the milking machines, and the gentle slurp of the milk as it finds it way to the sterile holding tanks. Where once there was the splendid grazing pasture land of Park Farm there now stands a new housing estate spreading its tentacles of roads over so much of what had once been an enormous back garden rich in its beauty and charm of an English rural setting. Another section of the village's agricultural past, the market garden, has also suffered, as its staff are tempted away from the land with the promise of higher industrial wages, and increased competition has made the localized growing of seasonal crops less profitable. With more money made from selling the land for building as the urban spread begins to gain momentum, so many of the local market gardens have passed into history, leaving acres of private houses standing on land which not so long ago gave us a harvest of root crops, top-growth vegetables, and succulent fruits of the summer.

Before the field pattern in and around Longwell Green changed forever, and before advances had been made to medical knowledge, country folk found herbs in the fields and hedgerows as remedies for all sorts of ailments, including the making of ointments for the healing of sores, and lotions for inflamed eyes. It is recorded that one local enterprising man produced from the products of the hedgerow a 'never fail' cough mixture, although what it tastes like or how effective it was is not recorded, but in fairness to this entrepreneur in those days any relief was probably worth having.

Although the main cereal crop in the region was wheat, it was also possible to grow barley which was an important crop for the production of beers and ale. Still standing at Hanham Green is the old malt house, where for hundreds of years barley was turned and dried to become the malting grain for sale to local brewers. Set out below are notes on malting at Stratton's Malt house, Hanham Green which have been gleaned from the reminiscences of Miss F.E.Nurse:

"The business was bought by Robert Nurse during the late 1700's and remained in the same family for almost two hundred years until 1937. Another Robert, who was born in 1855, succeeded his father in the business, which was a financial success, enabling Robert Francis Nurse to have a new house built during 1866 in front of the old premises. Around two bushels (approximately 73 1ts.) of malt would produce a thirty six-gallon (164 1ts.) barrel of beer at a gravity of 1057 degrees, later adjusted to 1055 degrees. Up to 1880, any duty payable was calculated on the malt but in that year a beer duty of six shillings and three pence (just over 30p) was charged per barrel, and to ensure that the correct amount of duty was paid, Excise Officers had the right to visit the premises day and night and to test the specific gravity of the product. Robert Francis Nurse was a licensed brewer until his death in 1923, when his second son William Richmond Nurse took over the business for the next fourteen years. Following William's death in 1937, the business closed"

Away from the prying eyes of the Excise Officers, many local farmers' wives made a wine called Bee Wine, a very potent drink made from a certain white fungus which grew on trees. Once harvested, it was placed in jars with a mixture of water and sugar and allowed to ferment and mature into a delicious but rather vigorous homemade wine.

Moving from agriculture and the production of intoxicating drink, there was once an iron mill at Willsbridge which had been erected either on the site of or, close by the old manor house of Oldland, on a stream once known as Mill Clack brook but now called Warmley Brook. As it approaches Willsbridge from Oldland, the brook runs through Southwood Valley where, during the early 1700's, a certain John Pearsall arranged for the stream to be dammed at the mill head. In doing so a millpond was formed from the adjoining meadow and orchard then known as 'Swans Flat'. Around 1712, John Pearsall converted the mill so that it would be capable of rolling iron, especially hoop iron, and the mill, in this condition, was successfully operated by that family for many years. Almost one hundred years later, his successor, Thomas Pearsall, took out a patent on the 30 December 1801 in respect of his invention in applying hoop iron as the load-bearing material in the construction of roofs, especially those which covered a wide span. Previously, of course, such roofs were supported by timber framing which was not only heavy but also becoming increasingly expensive. In particular, Thomas decided that by using his method he could roof over quite wide areas of the London Docks enabling ships to be loaded and unloaded in the dry. Having gone to enormous expense and had the roof erected, Thomas Pearsall was financially destroyed when the whole roof collapsed a little while after its erection. This virtually brought an end to the rolling of iron at Willsbridge, but relics of old iron rafters made on that site have been found in several old cottages recently demolished in the area. With his iron works closed and his finances in ruin, Thomas retired to Bath where he died, in March 1825, a broken man. As far as the mill was concerned, it was sold in 1816 and converted into a flour mill

Robert Lucas Pearsall was probably one of the last of his family to leave the locality; certainly he was the last Pearsall to live at Willbridge House. During his sojourn there he became well known for his musical abilities, composing madrigals performed by the Bristol Madrigal Society. He also wrote a good deal of music for the Bitton church choir, which he trained, plus the Ballad *'Oh, who will o'er the Downs so free'* which is still played by local brass bands. Before retiring to Germany, Robert Pearsall sold the family home in 1851 to a Captain Robert Stratton, who subsequently castellated the house as can be seen today with mock battlements, which has led to the house becoming more commonly known as Willsbridge Castle.

Deeper into Southwood Valley in the direction of Oldland is a glen known as Catscliffe which, during the first half of the nineteenth century contained a stone quarry owned by William Caine, whose family ancestors had played a major part in the notorious Cock Road Gang. Now more respectable than his antecedents, he and later his son, dug stone out of the hill mainly by hand for some fifty years, and many of the existing old houses in the village contain flagstones cut from that quarry.

* * * *

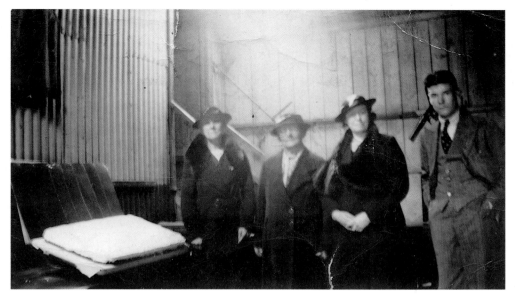

The Mothering Sunday simnel cake c1927

A family group 1900

LOCAL GOVERNMENT

A hundred years or so ago the village was so small that it was little more than a hamlet by-passed by its larger neighbours of Bitton, Oldland and Hanham Abbots, and unworthy of its own place of worship. As such when there was the need to control the ecclesiastical matters of the parish, Longwell Green's importance was well down (with apologies for the pun) the list of matters to be recorded. When Parish Councils first came into being it was decided that the old ecclesiastical boundaries were out of date so around 1894 new ones were proposed for the purpose of Local Government. As so often happens when committees get together to decide something on paper the practicalities of their decision is lost in the dust of the minutes, as was the reason why they decided to make the Bath Road part of the boundary between the parishes of Oldland and Hanham Abbots thus virtually cutting the village in half. Perhaps the line of the road was just too easy for them to ignore, in any case those who took the decision probably did not live in either half of Longwell Green, and therefore the decision was of no consequence to them. Whatever reason was debated, no one has seen fit to change the segregation and so it remains in existence today.

For much of the work carried out by the two parishes, such as footpaths; bad roads; bad pavements, overgrown hedges etc., the split of Longwell Green makes little or no difference, but as soon as the need arises for new amenities in the village, or a national celebration, then comes the added work of calling a joint parish council meeting so that the village can be treated as a whole. Yet it is still not just a question of an extra meeting as, each councillor has also to represent his own parish, thus they have to decide not only what is best or suitable for Longwell Green, but also how such a decision might affect their respective parish.

Under the chairmanship of Robert Francis Nurse, the first meeting of the Hanham Abbots Parish Council took place in January 1895, with high on the agenda the subject of how best they should act as the overseers of the Poor Law, and how they should arrange the collection of the rates. Other functions to be considered were the care and maintenance of footpaths and stiles. At their second meeting, the council needed to deal with a flood of applications applying for allotments which, considering the rural nature of the parish and the fact that most households would have had a reasonable size garden, no doubt came as quite a surprise. The applications certainly required the council to minute that they hoped to acquire land in the near future without having to resort to any form of compulsory order.

By the turn of the century the councils had a major preoccupation in the subject of roads and footpaths, which were the ultimate responsibility of Gloucestershire County Council, who held their meeting some forty-mile or so away in Gloucester City. It is of course worth remembering that at this time pavements were few and far between and the pedestrian either had to walk along the road itself or along the adjoining grass verge, which were very often dusty and uneven in summer and quite often muddy, slippery and dangerous in winter. In addition to these inconveniences, the majority of verges ran alongside ditches, which frequently overflowed in wet weather, and often became polluted with sewerage at any time during the year. The state of the roads, verges and ditches were accordingly a constant source of concern to the parish councillors, which led them to be continuously writing to the council in Gloucester City. Frustration led to frustration as their letters always seemed to meet with long delays before anything was done, and more often than not there were the same excuses then as there are today such as "the road/pavement cannot be repaired at present as the Water Company want to lay more pipes"

An interesting note, taken from the early days of the parish council and the subject of roads, follows a complaint made about the state of the road between Hanham Green and Crewe Green. Having considered the complaint, and having, no doubt, received a report upon the work required, the council decided that the road was to be repaired at a cost of not more than £4. A contractor offered to carry out the work by supplying twenty loads of stone at three shillings and nine pence (around 0.19p) per load, i.e. a total cost of £3.15.0 (£3.75p). Although the work was carried out for that price, the council reported some while later, that they were not very satisfied with the job as they had to spend £1, some seven years later, to put the work right.

Local interest was aroused during 1904 when it was heard that the Rural District Council had taken the decision to purchase a second-hand steam roller, action which the Hanham Abbots Parish Council were wholeheartedly in agreement with.

Another function of the council was to keep the village Post Office up-to-date, and as the population kept growing, so the councils continued applying for new services such as the sale of licences and postal orders; a public telephone; extra postal deliveries; and extra post (pillar) boxes. However somewhat like the roads, the simple submission of a request did not automatically generate a response, and it is recorded that these new and extra items certainly did not arrive as soon as the first or second application had been made, more often than not it took numerous requisitions before changes were made in the post office, and before a new public telephone kiosk was installed.

A housing committee was set up after the end of the Great War to consider if there was any need to expand the housing stock within the village, but after a certain amount of deliberation, the committee agreed that there were sufficient houses in the area to cope with the needs of the population. What a very different story emerged at the end of the Second World War. !!

In 1920 the question of a joint fire service with Kingswood arose, but in a rather typical local authority arrogant fashion of "we know best", the various parish councils would not agree to such a policy on the grounds that they, and they alone, considered the possibility of a fire breaking out, let alone one which might cause any damage, to be extremely remote. Six years later the risk of a fire had obviously increased, at least in the minds of the Hanham Abbots councillors, as they decided to purchase their own fire appliance and station, which consisted of a motorcycle, complete with a pump and a hose, and a wooden shed in which to house the equipment.

During 1929 the County Library in the Y.M.C.A. hut opened for business for the first time,

A Study of the minutes of the Annual General Meetings show, in quite a number of instances, that only the stated number of councillors put up for election, with those councillors who were elected going through on a show of hands. The idea of having secret ballots was not introduced until well into the current century.

During the thirty-eight years of its existence until 1933, the Clerk to the Hanham Abbots Parish Council had been Edwin Short, but after that length of service, Mr.Short decided that it was time for him to hand over to a younger man. Throughout the whole of those years, Mr.Short had only missed one meeting, and in recognition of his services, members of the Parish Council made a presentation to him.

Throughout the Second World War the councils assisted with the Air Raid Precaution department, and the fire fighting services, and had quite a big job organising the reception of evacuees from Bournville. With war clouds looming over Europe during the mid 1930's, it had been Government policy to try and identify areas within the Country, which were at risk from bombing, and those areas less at risk and which could therefore be considered to be a safe area. The village fell into the latter category and accordingly when war was declared, children from Birmingham were evacuated to the peace of Longwell Green. Although some of the children stayed for quite a while, the period of the phoney war when nothing much seemed to be happening on the 'Home Front' and certainly no German planes appeared in the sky above, the majority of the home-sick children returned home to the Midlands.

Towards the end of May 1939, and before the influx of the evacuees, the Parish Council persuaded the District Council to purchase, within the village, a piece of land to be developed as a playing field for children. Although the land was purchased, the war broke out before any work could be carried out and six years later the whole idea appeared to have been swept into the waste-paper basket.

As the war was beginning to come to an end, and local politicians and residents began to contemplate the "new and improved future", part of which was a suggestion that was brought to the councils meetings during 1944, that a village hall would be a most desirable asset for Longwell Green. Although considered by both councils, it was in fact a separate association that was formed to steer the idea through to completion. Not only did they perform this function, they have also taken over from the council the arranging of evening classes now held in the new village hall. As we bring ourselves up-to-date, today's council is now more concerned with such matters as the provision of bus shelters and wayside seats.

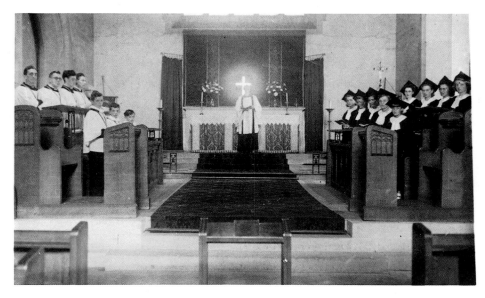

The Rev.K.R.Pilcher curate of All Saints' with choir 1950

A presentation is made to the Rev.K.R.Pilcher in August 1950 prior to his appointment as vicar of Alveston

The front of the YMCA carnival procession moving along Watson Road c1922

Ladies of the village enjoying a cup of tea during the summer garden party on the lawn of Harefield Hall 1934.

The start of a Sunday school outing either in 1924 or 1925

An enjoyable game of Hoop-la during the 1950 Field Day

The 1927 Temperance Queen and her entourage

One matter, which has given a growing and more modern population cause for concern, is the somewhat behind the scenes subject of sanitation. In 1925, the parishioners of Hanham Abbots Parish submitted a request to the council that the refuse should be collected and disposed of by the council. No doubt a reasonable, and almost certainly a sensible request but, as the Parish Council would have had to stand the cost of such a request, they understandably turned it down. Undeterred, the parishioners submitted further requests, but on each occasion the councillors did not consider that the cost warranted the benefits, assuming of course that a benefit of disposing of the refuse actually existed. The councillors representing the other half of the village obviously had a more modern approach to this problem and continued to lobby the Rural District Council (RDC) for financial help. By 1928 the Oldland Parish Councillors decided, as they were not likely to receive any help that they would set up their own collection. To a certain degree, this was little more than a bluff as the council were gambling on the fact that in view of the split boundary, they would force the hand of the RDC who had a responsibility for the whole village. Fortunately for the Parish Council the bluff worked and, by 1930, the District Council had set up a refuse collection, which covered the village and surrounding properties. Undoubtedly the service has improved over the past 28 years, but fundamentally it is the same service that was formed all those years ago, and the whole community has throughout that time benefited from the absence of unwanted articles being dumped in any odd corner of the village.

One of the other aspects of sanitation is the matter of drainage, particularly when cesspits and buckets were the order of the day. During the early 1930's the Government offered a 60% grant towards public works in contemplation, but not yet ready for immediate execution, and this led to a joint meeting being convened of all of the local parish councils, at which time they decided to bring pressure on the RDC to promote the establishment of main drainage in the centres of population including, of course, Longwell Green. Not unexpectedly, Warmley Rural District Council resisted the whole idea on the grounds of expense and the inability to pay. In addition, the senior council was also influenced by a report received from the Medical Officer of Health, who claimed that as the council would have to increase the level of rates to cover the council's share of the cost, that the increase would compel people to live in smaller houses which, in turn, would lead to increased overcrowding. Such a situation would, in the opinion of the Medical Officer, be worse than the absence of a sewer.

The more enlightened neighbouring Kingswood Urban District Council had by this time already established a sewerage system, with the required outfall works adjacent to Warmley Brook. After a while the stream became contaminated with untreated sewerage, and this gave rise to innumerable complaints and representations to the UDC and the Ministry of Health. An enquiry was ordered and as a result, the outfall works were condemned, leading Kingswood UDC to suggest a joint venture with Warmley RDC that, together, they should construct a mutual main trunk sewer scheme.

From 1930 onward, requests were continually made to the RDC for the main trunk sewer to be started, but incredibly throughout that decade not one pipe was laid, and whatever plans had been made, the start of the war caused the whole scheme to be completely shelved. With all plans held in abeyance during the duration of hostilities, the local parishioners had to wait until 1946 before they could call a special meeting to press for immediate action, although what they expected to happen, when sixteen years had past since the scheme was first considered, is not recorded. Not unexpectedly another year or more went by before the council were advised that an alternative sewerage scheme was in hand and under consideration by Gloucester, and that accordingly nothing could be done until that scheme had been properly consulted. Probably, had the village and its surrounding area retained the same level of population as it had pre-war, then it is more than likely that we would still be waiting for a main trunk sewer system to be installed but, with a great shortage of houses in Bristol, and the decision by Warmley RDC to help out by building a large housing estate at Park Farm, the need for a proper sewer system to be created became an imperative. During the early part of the 1950's the houses were built and the sewerage scheme was constructed and, at long last, in 1954 Longwell Green joined the twentieth century by being connected to the main trunk sewer, just twenty-four years after it was first proposed. Had the scheme been built in the first place then the cost would have been £66,000 of which, after the Government grant, just £26,400 would have had to be borne by the local ratepayer. As it was, the whole revised cost of £104,000 was met out of the local rates.

When the parish councils first began the village was still part of a very rural area with little or no community services of the type we today take for granted, including the lighting of streets. It must however be remembered that at the end of the nineteenth century very few houses would have any artificial light other than candle or possibly oil light. 1897 was the year in which Queen Victoria's Jubilee was celebrated, and as part of these celebrations, Mrs.E.Jefferies, who resided at Harefield Hall, arranged for three street oil lamps to be erected, two of which were sited within the Oldland Parish, one being by the Methodist Schoolroom and the other outside Oldland Hall, whilst the one in the Hanham Abbots parish was by Mr.W.Fry's yard. The cost of their erection and their maintenance was borne solely by Mrs.E.Jefferies throughout her lifetime, the parish council refusing to accept that street lighting was a necessity and that any cost incurred was a total waste of money on an unwarranted luxury. Accordingly as the lights were damaged, or became worn-out, the darkness of the night once again covered the whole village.

It was not until 1928 that the Rural District Council applied to provide public lighting, and subsequently the Warmley Electricity Company was formed, with the supply coming from a power station at Lydney. When, on the 15 March 1932, all of the newly erected street lights were switched on, Warmley RDC claimed to be one of the first rural districts in the country to have a comprehensive street lighting system, Having provided this new service for its ratepayers, part of the cost was met by the parish councils and, in an attempt to reduce the charge, a complaint was made by some of the councillors at one of their 1932 meetings, that the lights were being switched on too early in the evening and switched off too late in the mornings. At the same meeting it was also proposed that on moonlit nights the street lamps should not be switched on at all!!! All street lighting was of course non existent during the years of the war, not being switched back on again until 1945/46: however economies were still the order of the day which meant that for around the next ten years the lights went out at 11.0pm, being extended to midnight about a year or so ago.

* * * *

As already mentioned, the villagers and surrounding residents were in the past, totally dependent upon wells and springs to provide them with water, and it was not until the turn of the century that the West Gloucestershire Water Company piped water to the area. The source of supply was always of concern, and when California Pit closed in 1904, it was the Water Company that purchased the land and mine with a view of using the flooded workings as a form of underground reservoir. Although today the majority of people have water indoors, there are still a number of cottages in the area that have to rely upon outside garden taps.

* * * * *

COMMUNICATIONS

Historically country folk would try and take the most direct route possible when travelling between one point and another, which over the years became recognized footpaths. With the majority of people having to walk either to work, to church or even to socialize they naturally kept to the same paths throughout both parishes, and many of these footpaths are still in existence, and are legally created as a right of access. A stroll over the hills around Longwell Green and Hanham Green will show a network of these footpaths, many of which lead to St Anne's church and California Pit at Oldland, St George's Chapel at Hanham Abbots, and also to the pit at Memorial Road, the latter having been an important source of employment/income right up to the mid 1920's. Other paths have less well-defined starting/finishing points, but many will reflect the need for villagers to collect kindling and firewood. As recently as just twenty-five years ago or less, it was still a quite common occurrence to see inhabitants returning from the hills with arms full of sticks. The land around Mount Pleasant Farm holds numerous springs, which is another cause of some of the footpaths, although these might not be as well defined as those paths, which were used more frequently.

There is a well-worn footpath from Stonehill through one of the fields of Hinton Green Farm, skirting the Green and crossing two fields to Parkwall, which, since the coming of the Park Estate has become even more popular.

One path, which is known as "The Crack", appears to start/finish just opposite the *Butcher's Arms* and runs behind the Longwell Green Coachworks to Kingsfield Lane. Another one, known as "Drum Way", takes a route from Watson Road to Fry's Hill.

In addition there are a number of smaller footpaths, which are still in existence even though they may not take exactly the same route as they originally did. Farmers have not always been the friends of footpaths and walkers, and some have deliberately diverted the path from one field to another, especially when the other field belongs to a neighbouring farmer/land owner. For those whose use of the footpaths is less intrinsic, find that the tracks which lead up Stonehill to the 310ft. above sea level vantage point are able to enjoy beautiful views which stretch across the rural countryside to the Mendips in one direction, and the South Cotswold in the other.

Whilst the above paths are historical, there are other pathways, which have developed, in more recent years. Following the opening of Messrs. J.B.Fry & Sons, Chocolate Factory at Somerdale, local villagers have obtained employment there and they, together with pleasure seekers wishing to explore the delights of the river and surrounding areas, have helped to establish new routes. One of these lead over Westfield and the hills at the top of Willsbridge Hill, down to the River Avon, and thence along the towpath. This towpath is part of the Bristol to London long distance path scheme approved in 1956 by the Town Planning Committees of Wiltshire, Somerset, Bristol and Gloucestershire.

* * * *

The village, very obviously, is largely clustered around a main road leading from Bristol to Bath which follows the probable course of the old Roman road called Via Julia which ran from Bath to their nearest sea-port at Sea Mills. Until 1953 it had no specific name and had, for hundreds of years, just simply been identified as the 'main road', however in 1953 it was officially given the name Bath Road. As the road continues towards Bristol the name changes to Stonehill at the junction with Kingsfield Lane and, continuing along and past the *Blue Bowl Inn,* it is joined on the left-hand side, by Whittucks Road. If at this point, we turn left and continue down the road until it reaches the confluence of Memorial Road, Common Road and Abbots Road and then take the latter, which leads to Hanham Green, where it runs into Court Farm Road before meeting the main (Bath) road again at the top of Willsbridge Hill, we will have walk the approximate boundary of Hanham Abbots. A turning off Hanham Green is Castle Farm Road, which runs parallel to Common Road, both of which gradually dwindle into unmade lanes and then into footpaths taking the inquisitive wanderer into Hencliffe Woods. Beyond the junction with Castle Farm Road is the connection with Ferry Road, which leads the traveller to the *Chequers Inn.* At the end of this road the river can still be crossed by a ferry, which, since 1921, has belonged to the *Old Chequers Inne* then run by Mr.J.Whiting. Since then the ownership has changed on a number of occasions, and the premises are known as the *New Chequers Inn.* All of the roads mentioned above, were officially given their names in 1932.

Returning to the centre of the village, there are two other roads namely, Shellards Road and Watson Road, which, together with Bath Road form a triangle around the original green. Shellards Road begins at the Bakestone Café, previously the *Wheatsheaf Inn,* and which a few hundred yards further along is rejoined with Bath Road via Watson Road. Within living memory, these two roads were little more than muddy tracks, whilst Watson Road had fields on its Stonehill side. Approximately a quarter of a mile further on past the junction with Watson Road, Shellards Road meets, what used to be known as either Dodds Lane or more frequently Pit Lane, and which is now called California Road. Since the building of Park Estate, which stretches from this junction through to Warmley Tower, this narrow country lane has become a busy thoroughfare. California Road itself leads to the site of California Pit, and then on to St.Annes Church, or over the stream to Court Road, Oldland. Near to the site of the now disused pit is a track, which leads along the brow of the hill to the church and saves the need to drop down into the valley and then up again if the road is followed. Because of the steepness of the hill taking the road down to the level of the stream, it could become quite dangerous in bad weather by either being very slippery, or finding itself underwater at the bottom. Accordingly in the days of horse-drawn funerals, the cortege was quite often forced to use the track way to avoid the obstacles, which had been created by the elements on the road ahead.

Kingsfield Lane is a short cut to Kingswood which was frequently used before the war by residents involved with the boot and shoe trade, and by inhabitants wishing to shop in Kingswood, or even to catch the tram at the terminus, at the top of Hill Street.

Around 200 yards along Kingsfield Lane it turns quite sharply to the left and passes Hinton Green which is now the only surviving area of common ground in the village. For many years the lane was called Hinton Lane and during last year there was a certain amount of controversy as to whether or not it should be designated a road or a lane.

These roads have all, in some form or another, existed in living memory but in the past many have been known by different names, and by custom and habit many of the old names are still more frequently used by inhabitants of forty years of age or more. It should not, for example, be forgotten that prior to 1932 Watson Road was Pound Lane; Court Farm Road was Lime Kiln Lane and California Road was Pit Lane all reflecting an industry and/or the purpose for which the road was originally constructed. Many discussions have been held over the past twenty or thirty years as old industries have died and new purposes for the roads created. In addition, time was taken on determining names for roads, which at that stage had no significant name at all. For example, during November 1939, Hanham Abbots Parish Councillors spent some while considering the name of the main road running through Longwell Green with a suggestion that the stretch of road from the junction with Hinton Lane to the top of Willsbridge Hill should be called All Saints Road. Having put forward this proposition to Warmley RDC it was rejected, and the subject of a name remained in abeyance for the next six years. Even after the War had ended, the councillors were still unable to agree and the official name of Bath Road did not come into existence until 1953. It is both, interesting and amusing to note that it was the then recently retired Postman that was asked to help determine the name, particularly as there was now a greater urgency for the increasing number of houses to be given a proper postal number. Very obviously no one else had such a good knowledge of the names of the residents and where they lived, even when their designation was as elusive as say Mrs.W.Smith, Longwell Green.

Field Lane, opposite Oldland Hall is the one unadopted road in the village. It leads to fields adjoining Mount Pleasant Farm and for many years was locally known as Watery Lane, no doubt because of the amount of land drainage from the surrounding hills which was carried through the lane particularly after a storm.

Thirty years or more ago the local roadways were much more uneven and rutted than they are today, and often there was a footpath on one side only which, prior to 1945, mainly consisted of a layer of earth and stones edged with undressed stones of varying sizes. On the left hand side of the main road going in the direction of Bristol, an intermittent pathway ran along the top of a bank with a ditch between it and the adjoining boundary wall and fields. Over the past thirteen years or so, the pathways have been improved and now there are proper footpaths on both sides of the main road and, in addition, the road has been widened opposite the Coachworks. In 1954, Shellards Road was also widened and fitted with pavements. Much of the stone used in improving the roadways has come from a stonebreaker who used to work at the junction of the main road and Stonehill outside of the ground now occupied by No: 80 Stonehill, this being the last residence on the hill.

The recently built housing estates now have their own network of roadways and when Warmley RDC built over Earlstone Park, they used existing field names when naming the roads. Accordingly on that estate you will find Rushy; Little Dowles; Great Dowles; Long Handstones and Far Handstones, many of which radiate directly or indirectly from the central road which as a crescent has taken its name from the park. In contrast, the private estate being built on the other side of the main road by Messrs. Wimpey on former Market Garden ground perpetuates such names as Pearsall; Ellacombe; Stanhope and other people of renown who have in the past been connected with this district.

* * * *

When Abraham Fussell decided in the 1880s, to re-open California Pit, and to try and extract quality steam coal from the Smith's Seam, he looked longingly over the valley at the disused dramway and wondered how he could connect his pit with that means of transportation. To do so, he needed to take the coal by rail to a point above the valley floor, where he could install an incline; down which loaded wagons were lowered whilst pulling empty wagons up to the top. Although the construction of an incline was an engineering feat in itself, the problem he had given his engineers and construction workers did not end there as there was still the hurdle of Warmley Brook to be crossed and then a steep climb of fifty feet or so to reach the level of the dramway itself. They overcame these problems by foreshortening the incline and building a massive arched bridge over the stream on level with the bed of the dramway. Thus, loaded wagons could now be lowered down the incline, allowed to run into the tramway junction, before being reversed and by horsepower taken through Willsbridge tunnel and across the road near to the top of Brockham Hill. The original dramway had formed part of the Avon and Gloucestershire Railway, which was constructed to allow coal wagons to be collected from pits as far away as Coalpit Heath, and to run under gravity to the river Avon at either Londonderry Wharf or Avon Wharf. Although the miners reached Smith's Seam some 2000 ft. below the surface, the amount of coal in a seam rarely exceeding 20 inches thick never produced the quantity of coal to make the pit economical and, like so many other pits in the area, California suffered from the continual problem of flooding. By 1904/05 there was so much water in the tunnels that the pit had to be abandoned, despite the fact that during the twelve or so years of it's operation, the output was probably never more than one load of around five coal trucks (50tons) per day, to be taken down to the river. However, because more than just coal had to be hacked out of the confined underground tunnels, the amount of material actually brought to the surface was probably nearer 60-70 tons per day.

Although the dramway was designed for the wagons to roll forward under gravity, a horse was placed at the front of a rake of trucks predominantly to act as the main form of braking, the only other braking system employed being a man, with a long stick, who walked alongside the trucks and whose job it was to thrust the stick between the spokes of the wheels, in the hope that this would bring all of the wagons to a stop.

Once across Brockham Hill the wagons were shunted into Willsbridge Wharf where the coal was graded into size and then sent either by Londonderry Wharf for onward shipment by barge to Bristol, or by crossing the Keynsham Road in a tunnel to Avon Wharf, and onward shipment to Bath and beyond.

* * * *

During the month of May 1897, an application was made by the Bristol Tramways and Carriage Co. Ltd. in pursuance of the Light Railway Act 1896 for an Order to authorise the construction of a Light Railway from Summerhill Road in the City and County of Bristol, to Hanham in the parish of Kingswood in the County of Gloucestershire. Although covered by the Light Railway Act, the Company were applying to extend their existing electrical tram system, and work started on this line during the early part of 1899, with the route opened on the 22 December 1900. As the early years of the twentieth century passed, it was shown that this novel means of public transport was extremely popular, and consideration was given to extending the line from Hanham through to Bitton, which would obviously have taken it through the main road at Longwell Green. Regrettably, this proposal never came to fruition and it was left to Mr.W.Bence to inaugurate a local bus service over the following years to come.

As far as a main railway was concerned, the nearest system to reach Longwell Green was when the Midland Railway constructed a branch line from Mangotsfield to Bath and opened a station at Bitton, which, fortunately, still provides us with the nearest railway station and a means of getting to Bath by public transport.

* * * *

At the turn of the century horses were still the main motive power of transport, and horse buses operated between Longwell Green and Hanham during the 1870s to 1890s. On occasions, some of those buses or certainly a change of bus would continue on to Bristol terminating at the *White Hart Hotel in* Old Market Street. A number of these buses were owned by George Flook who lived in the house now called "Windsor" opposite the Butchers Arms, and by a Jessey Grey and William Kendall. The buses used, carried around 12 or 14 passengers and looked rather like a cross between a bakers van and a gypsy caravan. One of the last of these vehicles could be seen for many years in a garden in Kingsfield Lane, where it spent a number of years in retirement, firstly as a playhouse and then a tool shed before being broken up about four years ago.

William Kendall was also involved in his family firm, which was based in Church Road, Hanham, and operated a horse drawn carrier service from Bristol via Longwell Green to Bitton. As far as can be determined, this service began around 1870, and used as a collection/dropping point for both passengers and goods the *Wheatsheaf Inn* at Longwell Green the *Blue Bowl* at Stonehill and the *Maypole* at Hanham. Mr. Kendall was also a heavy goods haulier of stone, timber, coal and cattle feed, but it appears that this side of his business was handed over to his son, Ernest, around 1900. The family continued to use horse drawn vehicles in and around the area until the mid-1920s when they gradually replaced our equine friends with more modern petrol driven lorries.

As the motor vehicle became more reliable and more accessible, the public realised that they could now travel much further in a day than had previously been possible by horse-drawn brakes. A day-trip to somewhere like Weston-S-Mare at the turn of the century usually involved a three or four hour journey each way on hard wooden seats, with little or no other comfort on the brake itself, and probably no cover against the vagaries of our unpredictable weather. That is not to say that those who were able to go did not enjoy themselves, as such a trip, however uncomfortable to our modern eyes, could still be one of the highlights of the year. Those who manufactured lorry chassis were, especially after the First World War, quick to see that by putting bench seats across the chassis, surrounding the vehicle with a series of access doors, and fixing a canvas hood over the whole vehicle, which could be folded back on warm dry summer days, could create a more comfortable means of transporting a number of people to the same destination and back. Thus was born the charabanc, and the extension of the day-trip, a new and novel way of taking 30 or more people together either to the seaside, a mystery tour or to places of interest. This new mode of transport did not pass by the village or the owner of Glentworth Garage, who operated from the premises now occupied by H.C.Hardwick Ltd., as he soon obtained a Peerless motor lorry equipped with wooden slatted seats and began to run day-trips to the seaside at Weston. Although still somewhat uncomfortable it was virtual luxury compared with the horse-drawn brake seating and, in any case, the journey time was fewer than half that it had been when real horsepower was being used. To be dropped off along the promenade at Weston, well in time for a morning drink and stroll, followed by a hearty lunch of fish and chips and an afternoon relaxation on the beach was the dream of many who lived in the area, who rarely had a day away from the constant drudgeries of work. After a day at the seaside where you could let your hair down! who cared about the journey home on hard wooden seats, and a vehicle with solid tyre wheels. Incidentally one of these seats can still be tested for comfort at the Y.M.C.A. hut, where it is still in common use. With the success of the day-trip business, the old Peerless lorry soon gave way to a new thirty-two seat open charabanc, complete with the much improved red leather sprung cushion seating and a canvas hood. In such additional luxury the residents of Longwell Green could travel to Weston-Super-Mare and back in a day, all for the princely sum of two shillings (0.10p).

During the early part of this century, William J.Bence was a local wheelwright, and part-time undertaker, operating from the premises now occupied by the Longwell Green Coachworks. At the time the main source of income for any skilled wheelwright, including Mr.Bence, was from the craft of manufacturing spoked wooden wheels, and wooden bodies, to be fitted to any type of horse-drawn vehicle. However, it was becoming increasingly obvious that horsepower was going to suffer in the future from a great deal of competition from the new fangled mechanical power, bursting on to the unsuspecting public as the twentieth century unfolded. As far as this particular wheelwright was concerned, changes needed to be made if he was going to benefit from this new technology and accordingly, he gradually began to diversify and expand his business to include the manufacture of bodies for commercial motor vehicles. However the traditional skills of being a wheelwright were not completely abandoned until the early-mid 1930's.

William Bence was certainly an enterprising man as, not only was he a wheelwright as described above, he had in addition, during the last few years of the nineteenth century, set up a carriers' business operating from a variety of villages such as Doynton, Bitton, Hanham and of course, Longwell Green into Bristol, and as a carrier he not only transported goods he also encouraged the carrying of passengers. As his empire expanded, he invited his two sons Henry and Albert to join the business, changing the name to W.J.Bence & Sons. Subsequently, and due to the success of the passenger-carrying venture, combined with the body building business, W.J.Bence & Sons began to build bus bodies onto supplied chassis, including the building of buses for their own bus company, Bence Motor Services that was established during the early 1920's. At its peak, this company owned some twenty-five or thirty buses, driven by men who still wore leggings and breeches. The earlier buses had solid tyres, and two or three much sought after seats beside the driver. The signal bell was fixed to the roof over the driver's head, and hand operated by the conductor, at the back, by the use of a lead, which ran along the underside of the roof, being attached at intervals by eyelets. All of the buses operated by the Motor Service had a green livery, similar to that currently used by the Bristol Tramway Company, but had white window frames instead of cream, and a white painted roof.

There were no bus stops in between the fare-stages, as these would seem to be a comparatively modern invention having first started to appear during the autumn of 1943, thus anyone wishing to stop the bus simply hailed it from the road side, where ever they happened to be. Similarly you asked the conductor to ring the bell a few moments before you wished to alight. There were times when the owner and/or the management wished to stop the bus, and this was usually done by setting an empty petrol tin at the roadside to attract the driver's attention. Having stopped the bus, the conductor would run into the office for instructions, which might be to pick-up a passenger, or parcel from an isolated house/farm for onward delivery, or a prospective passenger might accompany the conductor back to the bus to be conveyed to its destination. This helpful efficient and friendly service linked the surrounding villages of Keynsham, Bitton, Oldland, Warmley, Hanham, Willsbridge and Kingswood. However as with all bus services it was not with out its problems and, quite a few people living in Longwell Green today, can remember getting off a bus when it came to such places as Willsbridge Hill, and lending a hand at the back to help push the bus over that obstacle.

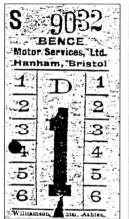
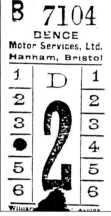

Fares could be paid in cash to the conductor on the bus, or by means of tickets previously purchased in book form from the company's office. Penny tickets were usually white, with the colour pink reserved for the more expensive two-penny tickets. At that price, it was not unknown for some people to purchase the tickets on the 'pay a bit/owe a bit' system.

As the second decade of the century began to close, the more powerful and larger neighbour of Bristol Tramways & Carriage Co Ltd. continued with their expansion, including the merger of the Bath Electric Traction Co, and on the 5 November 1928, fireworks began to spark when Bristol started its country service to Bath via Bitton and in doing so immediately crossed Bence's territory. To start with the occasional through bus did not make a great deal of difference. Most people gravitated to Bristol for their special shopping and accordingly continued to catch one of Bence's buses to Hanham, and then transferred to an electric tramcar that took them into the heart of the city. For a few years both companies worked side by side as best they could but with the larger company able to play a waiting game whilst at the same time able to afford financial incentives to try and persuade passengers to use their services, Bence Motor Services were finding it harder and harder to make ends meet. By the early to mid 1930's, negotiations were under way between both companies and on the 1 July 1936 the inevitable happened, and the smaller company was totally swallowed by their powerful neighbours from next door.

With so many men away at the front during the First World War, two enterprising young ladies, one of whom was William Bence's daughter Letitia, with the other being Mabel Gough whose father, George Gough, owned the *Butcher's Arms,* considered that there would be a need in the village and surrounding area for a private hire car service to be implemented, and accordingly they jointly invested in a Ford Model 'T' car. Bearing in mind how unusual it was ,in those days, for ladies to drive let alone to go out and work for a living, these two young women must have had a great deal of courage to start what they did, although how successful they were was never recorded.

According to the now retired local market gardener Albert Gully, his father Thomas who built the Almshouses and the Methodist Schoolroom was, in his day, a pioneer of steam wagons in the Bristol area. One of these steam driven wagons was used daily by Albert to haul manure from the many stables in Bristol to Mr.W.Fry's market garden. However, he remembers that this particular vehicle was not altogether successful as it frequently broke down. Despite Albert's experience many steam wagons were built by the Company Foden and were to be seen in general use until the late 1920s. As the petrol driven lorry became more reliable, they gradually replaced the steam wagons which themselves had over the years been the cause of a number of accidents, very often due to the excessive amount of smoke they made, so impairing the vision of other motorists.

* * * *

For many years which straddled 1900, letters were delivered on foot by a local character by the name "snuffy" Jenkins who walked in all winds and weathers, and whose nickname was much more prevalent when those winds blew from a cold direction. Despite Mr. Jenkins' impediment he rarely failed to deliver all of the mail before breakfast. After snuffy Jenkins retired, his round was taken over by Walter Jefferies, who carried out his duties with the aid of a bicycle and, as previously mentioned, assisted the Parish Council in identifying the houses when the roads were officially named and the houses officially numbered. There was one delivery daily until after 1945, and for many years up to 1936 only one collection of mail from the sole collecting box situated at the Post Office. Later in that year, a collecting box was erected in the wall of the Longwell Green Coachworks and was one of the few in the country, which had the Edward VIII cipher, embossed upon it. This was replaced just after 1945 with a George VI ciphered box and, at the same time, other boxes were fitted in the wall of Harefield Hall and at Parkwall.

* * * *

One of the first telephones to be installed in the village was rented by William J Bence, on a party line, which he had to share with five other subscribers. Anyone wishing to use the 'phone had to take off the receiver, leaving the mouth piece in a fixed position, either on a table or fixed to a wall, and if they could hear someone talking they knew that the line was not clear and had to wait before they were able to call the Exchange and ask for the number they required. This 'phone was not fitted with a dial and to call the Exchange they had to ring a bell by turning a handle at the side of the instrument. In those days only the Exchange had a means of dialling out a number. With six subscribers to the one line, lengthy telephone calls had to be avoided at all cost if the relationship between these subscribers was to be kept as friendly as possible. Subsequently, the first all-in-one hand set appeared on the scene which was a great improvement over the earlier model, even though it was necessary for the caller to keep his/her fingers firmly on the bar in the middle for the connection to remain open.

The use of a telephone right up to the late 1930s was very much the privilege of a few, especially in the village, which did not have its first public telephone kiosk until 1936, and this was only erected outside of the Post Office after considerable pressure by the District and Parish councils.

* * * *

As this century developed the availability of newspapers for the general public increased and over the years the demand for more news quickly introduced a number of daily papers either published for morning consumption or evening consumption. As far as the residents of Longwell Green and Hanham Green were concerned, the absence of a newsagent trading in the area meant that their newspapers needed to be delivered either from Hanham or from Bitton. From around 1926 to just prior to the start of the Second World War, Mr. Payne was the local agent. He had formerly been a collier at Hanham Pit but having retired from that job he set about delivering papers even though he did not own a shop. By all accounts Mr. Payne was quite a character as, whilst delivering the papers, he would very often shout in a loud voice to let people know he was coming and, later, when his rheumatism made it difficult for him to get around, he would whilst standing at the customer's gateway shout out that he was there and wait for the householder to fetch the paper.

Saturday sports fans are catered for by a Bristol newsagent who brings the edition of the Green'Un and the Pink'Un to the village where little groups of people would wait for him at appointed places such as the corner of Watson Road and by the Church. This practice has been going on for the past ten or eleven years.

* * * *

The inhabitants of Longwell Green have never been afraid of trying out new inventions, especially with each phase of the aerial entertainment, starting with the old cats whiskers wireless crystal set and gradually moving on through the radio to commercial television. This has been evident from the outward signs since the early 1920's when radio aerials, some resembling multiple clotheslines, first began to appear. These have now been taken over by the more modern forest of complicated aerials which began to appear in 1948 for the reception of BBC television and which have thickened over the past year or so following the opening, in 1957, of commercial television. Even before the latest transmitter at Wenvoe opened, television aerials appeared above the chimneystacks, with most owners claiming that the reception was very good.

* * * *

RELIGIOUS ACTIVITIES

Prior to 1896 there was no place for members of the Church of England to worship in Longwell Green instead, the villagers who wished to attend church either had to walk to St Anne's at Oldland, or St George's Chapel at Hanham Abbots. The former, had originally been a Chapel of Ease to the mother church at Bitton, and was probably constructed sometime during the eleventh/twelfth centuries, as certainly there is a mention of the chapel in documents dated 1220, which are held by the Worcester Cathedral Archives. Due to the condition of its structure, the original building was taken down in 1830, and replaced with the one that can be seen today. An Ecclesiastical District of St.Anne's Oldland was formed out of the Parish of Bitton, by an order of Council dated June 26th, 1861, and from then on Oldland has been a separate Parish.

Those villagers who wished to travel even further afield for their religious activities could either attend St. Mary's at Bitton, or Christ Church Hanham, the latter having been consecrated on October 18th. 1842, by Bishop Monk, becoming a separate Parish from Bitton on March 4th, 1844. Previous to 1817, the religious well being of all of the inhabitants of the area mentioned above, and also a great deal of the district surrounding these parishes, came under the sole responsibility of the Vicar of Bitton. However in 1817, his burden was lightened with the appointment of a joint curate to St.Anne's and St.George's, an arrangement that continued until the creation of the new parishes. There have been burials in the churchyard at Oldland since 1719, whilst the birth and marriage register dates from 1686, with many of the signatures only being identified by an X.

However, back to Longwell Green, and the final years of the nineteenth century when the increasing number of inhabitants were making arrangements, to have their own place of worship. Accordingly, sometime around 1896/97, a corrugated iron structure, known as the Tin Church, was erected and dedicated, and used for all licensed services until All Saints' Church was built at the beginning of this century. John Lysaghts of Bristol constructed the Tin Church on the 'Green' with money raised by donations from local subscribers, a grant from the Bishop of Bristol's Church Extension Committee, and an exceptional gift of money from Mrs.E.Jefferies of Harefield Hall. To honour and acknowledge the generous help of this lady and her family, there is a tablet in the church with the following inscription: –

"The Chancel, South Chapel and three Bays of the Nave and South Aisle of this church were erected A.D.1908 at a cost of £4,342, of which sum £3,000 were contributed from the estate of the late James Tolman, through the kind interest of Mrs.Jefferies and the late David Jefferies of Harefield Hall of this parish and the goodwill of Alfred Somerville Dodson, trustee of the estate".

There are in existence, management committee minutes which date from 1905, including the entry, which reads that an extra £10 was needed to purchase land from a certain Mr.Nurse for the new church.

The plans of All Saints, to be constructed by Messrs.Long of Bath, were first shown to the Church Committee at a meeting at Harefield Hall in June 1907, when the cost of building was estimated to be in the region of £3,400. With the plans approved, and most of the money raised, construction started in earnest with the laying of the foundation stone on October 12th 1907. A photograph of this ceremony can be seen in the vestry. Amongst the enthusiasm and delight, that at last the village was to receive a 'properly built church' of its own, there were one or two in the village who had their doubts that there were likely to be constructional problems in the years to come. Whilst the church was being constructed the man in charge very often lunched at the home of Mr.Gray who, from his local knowledge of the area and the land on which the church was being built insisted that one of the walls of the church would collapse, stating *"I sha't see it but my little maid will"*. His reasoning was that the wall was being built over one of the wells of the Green which had not been properly filled in. Interestingly, his 'little maid' still lives in the village, and the wall has subsided, so whether his prophecy will come true or not still hangs in the balance.

All Saints, a daughter church of St.Anne's Oldland, was licensed and opened in 1908, Interestingly, the church building is right on the boundary line separating the parishes of Oldland and Hanham Abbots, whilst the village itself is almost split in two by both parishes, although a small part is actually situated within the Parish of Kingswood.

During 1912, there was an attempt to sell off the Church Room, the Church being as it frequently was, very short of financial funds. How serious the attempt was, or what sorts of enquiries were received is not recorded, all that we know is that the Church Room still exists today.

In 1913, just five short years after it had been constructed, the church was in need of repair, at a cost of £38.2.5 (£38.12p) to its west wall, (the start of Mr.Gray's prophecy?). Certainly, there has, since that time, been a continual need for repairs, and we can only hope that the recent restoration of the Church will end the need for fabric repairs for some time to come.

With the First World War having intervened, it was some six years later when it was felt that the oil lighting in the church was inadequate, and accordingly more lamps, at a total cost of £15 were installed, with two of them being equivalent to at least 150-candle power. Although the new lamps must have been an improvement they did not solve the lighting problem as, a year or so later, £100 was spent taking out the old oil lighting and replacing it with gas lighting. This form of lighting continued over the next decade or so, but by 1931 the parishioners were looking for ways of improving the illumination given out by gas lamps. With the obvious way being to change over to the much brighter electric lighting, a proposal was made that electric lighting should be installed in the church as soon as possible. However admirable this proposal was, there was one very important matter which had been overlooked by those who had put it forward and that was that, at the time Longwell Green was still awaiting the arrival of mains electricity, and accordingly, a little red-faced, the proposal had to be withdrawn. As the years rolled by, and this country once again found itself at war with Germany the chance of dusting down the proposal was lost for fifteen years, and it was not until 1946 that the question of electricity being installed in the church was once again considered. Raising the question and carrying out the work was never likely to be consecutive, and it took a further three years before electric power was installed in the church, which subsequently enabled the much improved lighting to be switched on, plus allowing an electric blower for the organ to be installed, all for the complete cost of £270.

Around the same time that the lighting was first being changed, consideration was being given to the erection in the church of a brass plaque War Memorial, honouring the eighteen men from the village and surrounding areas who made the supreme sacrifice in Flanders and in other battlefields of the First World War.

By now the benefactress Mrs.E.Jefferies, had died and in her Will she left All Saints a legacy of the interest arising from £500 War Loans, on condition that a small sum be paid annually from the church funds, but not from the income from the legacy to Bristol Cemetery Company for the upkeep of the Jefferies' Vault at Arnos Vale Cemetery.

During the next few years little changed with hardly any alterations being carried out to the church. The community was however, fortunate inasmuch as the curate in charge appeared to be a 'dab hand' at woodwork, as a new notice board and a memorial table, to place beneath the War Memorial plaque, were both made by him.

The only other changes of note, was the construction of a porch, the erection of a flag-pole, and the installation of eleven new pews, manufactured by England & Son of Oldland at a cost of £70.10.0 (£70.50p)

During 1928, an appeal fund was started to raise money for the restoration of the Chancel floor and wall; a house for the priest in charge, and a stone built hall for parochial purposes. The amount needed to complete these proposed projects was estimated to be in the region of £2,400. Yet some thirty years after the launch of the appeal, only the restoration of the Chancel floor and wall has been completed. All Saints' is still using the Tin Church of the late nineteenth century as a Church Hall, and the present curate is living in a council house on the nearby estate.

The year after launching the appeal, Longwell Green experimented for a year at being an independent conventional district, but this was obviously not considered a wise move, as the final step was never taken.

A visit was made to the church during 1931 by the Diocesan Architect who reported that despite the fact that the building was only twenty-three years old, urgent structural repairs were needed to be undertaken, the first of which was the relaying of the Chancel floor and the reconditioning of the Sanctuary, followed by necessary repairs to the west wall.

The incumbent during the 1930's, was very eager to see the setting up of a children's corner around the font, and this was eventually put in place with the help of money raised by the Sunday school, and partly by a children's concert. Other fund raising activities took place with one, which was started by an anonymous gift of £5, subsequently paying for the wooden screen in the vestry to be constructed by pupils of the Kingswood Reformatory School.

The heating of the church has apparently never been satisfactory, with various minutes being recorded with regard to either the inadequacy or incompetence of the equipment, which continued even after the system was overhauled in 1933. Bad church attendances, particularly during the winter months, were frequently blamed on the absence of any real warmth.

The Diocesan Architect made another inspection of the building in 1945 and considered that urgent repairs were required to the Chancel Arch, and that the Vestry wall needed to be re-plastered. Within a matter of months both jobs had been carried out at a price of £210.9.8. (£210.50p), money raised by using the Legacy, the Appeal Fund, and with some help from St.Anne's and the Diocesan Board of Finance.

From 1946, discussions were held with regard to the War Memorial, and how best to include the names of those who had fallen during the war just ended. This matter however, did not just concern those responsible for the church but the whole village, as the Chapel, the Memorial Hall and the Playing Fields Association were all contributing. Some of those involved considered that the new memorial should be made of stone; others thought wood or brass were better mediums to honour the dead of two World Wars. In the end it was decided that the original First World War plaque should be scrapped and that in its place there should be a stone memorial containing the eighteen names from the first conflict, plus the names of the six men from the village who had died during the recent war. Having raised the money, the stone was duly carved and dedicated in 1952.

By 1951 the heating situation in the church had become close to being desperate, and the authorities were faced with the choice of either installing a completely new system at a cost of £600, or having a new boiler fitted, and utilising parts of the old system at half the cost. Perhaps not surprisingly they opted to spend just £300.

The following year, with the war well and truly over, a metaphorical bombshell fell on All Saints' when, after another visit by the Diocesan Architect, who was accompanied by a builder, members of the church were horrified to be told that the fabric of their church was in such a perilous state that it was likely to cost at least £2,000 to put matters right. Such an amount seemed well beyond their individual or collective reach, but they knew that the church definitely met a need in the life of

Longwell Green, and accordingly the building had to be saved at all cost. The first work to be undertaken was the exterior repairs, which had originally been estimated at £600, but when the final bill was presented, the actual cost was considerably less and, because of this factor, the account was settled from donations, and a generous gift made appropriately on All Saints' Day. With money tight, matters moved fairly slowly, so that it was 1954 before the next few jobs were carried out, including the redecorating, repairing and the colour washing of the Chancel and Vestry at a cost of £370. Two years later a local builder, at a cost of £570, redecorated the Nave, whilst the Parish Church paid to have the organ renovated.

During 1956, another gift day was organised which brought in a total of £135 for the Restoration Fund. Other fund raising activities included collecting boxes, bazaars and jumble sales, with generous gifts from the Parish Council and from individuals, including one person who anonymously donated a pair of new gates when the boundary wall was being repaired and repointed. Other material gifts included a new hymn board from the Men's Club, plus new churchwarden staves; new curtains for the vestry screen; new hymn books; a new altar book, dedicated *'In memory of departed loved ones'*. Almost certainly, this means that over the past five years approximately £2,400 has been spent on All Saints', the bulk of which was raised by the church members themselves in various ways, and was in addition to the running cost of the church. With all of the interior decorations completed in 1956, Dr.F.A.Cocin, the Bishop of Bristol, was invited to preach in the church on the All Saints Patronal Festival.

Normally, All Saints' has a curate in charge that works with and under the vicar of St.Anne's, Oldland. However during the six year period from 1950 to 1956, there was no curate in office which meant that there was a great deal of extra work for the parish vicar, the revision of the times of service, and an influx of many more lay readers than normal. All of these problems were occurring at the same time that Parkwall was being built and occupied by an ever-enlarging number of parishioners, thus the appointment of Mr. Francis Gill as the new curate was very welcome.

It is somewhat difficult to estimate the number of parishioners who actually attended church as people's memories and ideas vary so much. However the number of people who attended the Annual General Meetings can give some indication and, as one might expect, these figures show a fall during the war years gradually increasing thereafter.

In 1929, the choir consisted of twelve men, eight boys and six girls. There were ten Sunday school teachers and Miss.R.Baber, a primary school teacher who acted as a Superintendent. This lady had become a teacher in Bristol, and under her, the Sunday school flourished so that by 1933 there were 130 pupils in the school, an exceptionally high number for the size of the village at that time. The following year, the number attending had increased to 140, of which 65 were classified as infants. This was possibly the peak of Sunday school attendance which, with minor variation, continued until 1937 when Miss Baber retired. Such was her influence that after Miss Baber's retirement, Sunday school numbers began to drop and it is only recently, and mainly as a result of the building of the council estate, that the numbers have once again reached 100. Regrettably no permanent Register of Sunday school attendances have been kept, although one has been traced for 1923, which also records the existence during that year of a kindergarten, but since that date it is impossible to trace any records right through. Considering the number of pupils attending Sunday school, it is surprising to note that for the same period of time the average number of persons on the Electoral Roll seems to have been as low as 108 and only as high as 129.

One of the reasons why there may have been above average attendance in the choir and Sunday school, may be due to the annual outings which occurred from 1920. There is a record that in 1928 the choir went to Teignmouth for the day at the cost of 8/6d each (£0.42½). In those days there were even outings for the Sunday school teachers. Not all treats incurred trips to the seaside, some of the existing Church members recall an annual Sunday school event where the children went to Mr. Colston Fry's market garden and in sheds which had been whitewashed for the occasion, the children were provided with strawberry teas. This event went on for many years during the 1920s, but on one occasion, the Sunday school was taken to Dyrham Park by brakes and it was recalled that all of the children and accompanying adults had to get out at the bottom of Tog Hill and walk to the top, it being too steep for the horses to pull a loaded brake. By 1929, the Sunday school outings were more adventurous with a daytrip to Weston-super-Mare, including afternoon tea. However, in 1957, new heights were reached, and the Sunday school went to Barry Island by train.

A noted celebration in the Church during the 1930s took place on Mothering Sunday. At that time, the Mothers Union mixed a Simnel cake, which was taken to Hales Bakery at Hanham for baking, whilst Jason Billing & Sons, market gardeners at Stonehill, supplied violets and everyone attending the Church on that Sunday received a piece of cake and a bunch of violets.

On Remembrance Sunday afternoon a united service is held, usually at the Church, with the Methodists and the Brotherhood congregations present. Also in attendance are the Guides, Scouts and Cubs and both the minister and the vicar take it in turns to take the service and give the address. Attendance at the Remembrance service is excellent and it is nice to know that we can all unite in common worship on occasions such as this. This coming together of different denominations started with the intercessional united prayers, held on Wednesday evenings, during the war years.

During the mid-1920s there were numerous calls for unity within the Church, with the vicar at the 1937 Annual General Meeting complaining that the numbers attending were very unsatisfactory, and he put the cause down to the warm weather, the increasing use of the wireless and also disinclination to religious practice. It is interesting to see that he partially laid the blame on the existence of the wireless, which today is no doubt aided and abetted by the further distraction of television.

Perhaps the vicar's words did not entirely fall upon deaf ears, as it is noted that there were 1,018 Communicants in 1938, but the vicar was a difficult man to please, and he still felt in his communication that the district was one, which seemed so careless and indifferent to religion.

In addition to the drop in Sunday school attendance, the girls' Bible Class had faded out through lack of leadership and around the same time the Mothers Union was also dissolved. The support of the Church with active attendance apparently became steadily worse, as at another AGM where the Chair was taken by the rural Dean, he also expressed his concern by the low attendance at that meeting, plus also the lack of support at the Church services, which he considered was also due to the lack of reverence. By the time that the rural Dean was making his comments, it appeared that the choir had also been disbanded. Fortunately, since the end of the war, there has been an improvement in the support of the Church and those attending, and there is now a well-balanced Church choir which endeavours to give a lead in the Church worship.

In 1920, the first ladies' committee was formed, but it was the following year before one of those ladies sat on the management committee. With the emancipation of women gradually gaining understanding there was, in 1933, a suggestion that the choir be expanded with the inclusion of the female voice. Both ladies and girls were quick to take up this suggestion and enhanced the Church choir over the coming years. From 1939 onwards, there were many more ladies on the management committee and almost certainly it was the women of the village who, left behind at the outbreak of war, kept the Church going during those dark hours. Of course, during the war, Church service times had to be altered, as it was impossible to adequately create a 'proper blackout' situation. Discussions raged throughout the winter months as to whether or not an afternoon service should be held in the Church, or to retain the traditional evening service, but to hold it in the Church Hall, which did have adequate blackout.

As the war took a firmer grip on the country the 1940 Garden Party was postponed owing to the grave situation and the threat of invasion: even the Parish magazines were delayed owing to enemy action. An accountant, who acted as auditor, resigned as he was too busy with war service. By 1942 the price of oil was now 50% higher than it had been at the outbreak of war, and although the ladies did their utmost to continue with the normal functions of the Church and the fund raising activities, their bazaars and garden parties all suffered from the lack of goods. By 1944 the Church Hall was being used for such events as fireguard and fund raising activities to assist the war effort. However, there were those in the community who were looking to the future, and felt that appeals should be launched to help build churches on post war estates. A community association was formed in the village, with a view to building a Memorial Hall but, whilst the Church realized the value of such an undertaking, it felt that it simply could not further increase it's financial responsibilities, having already been committed to the rebuilding of the men's' club.

Local servicemen returning home were sent a card of welcome, and it was suggested that all churchgoers might like to make a thanks offering for the preservation of those who were returning. Sadly there was one notable absentee, the vicar's son, who had been killed in action during 1944.

With the war over, All Saints found itself without a curate in charge. However, the vicar was very interested in young people and did much to encourage them to attend church. Under his encouragement, a flourishing youth fellowship was built up, with young people taking, once a month, as much as possible of the service, this included the reading of the lesson, taking collections, choosing hymns and acting as sidesmen. Quite frequently there would be up to fifteen or twenty teenagers in the congregation, in addition to those in the choir, compared with the usual three or four.

One of the many new challenges facing the Church community after the war was how they could welcome and deal with the influx of families from the Bristol blitz. The Sunday school numbers had increased a great deal but as yet, the effect on Church attendance was only felt at the greater festivals, with little interest being shown with regard to other Church activities.

* * * *

Although the above has concentrated upon the Church of England, other denominations have had their place of worship in the village. Certainly, a chapel was the first place of worship to be built in Longwell Green, and it is understood that during the early eighteenth century a Wesleyan chapel stood on the site of the present Methodist chapel. This is predominantly a Nonconformist area especially after John Wesley had used one of the nearby hills as his preaching summit to the ungodly miners of Kingswood, and it is therefore quite feasible that the early chapel was, itself, used by this Evangelist during his preaching tours. There are many stories concerning John Wesley, George Whitfield and various Baptist preachers connected with the surrounding area, although none can be specifically identified with this village. John Wesley is, of course, the most famous of those who preached in the area and he is known to have converted a great many of the miners who at that time were reputed to be very wild and unruly. It was, of course, not only miners who were ungodly and thus many of those who inhabited Longwell Green and the surrounding area would have been affected and influenced by the preaching of these religious men. So great was the influence of Wesley, that as part of the 1951 Festival of Britain celebration an outdoor pulpit and beacon were erected in his memory on the hill now known as Mount Hill. Every night, winter or summer, the green beacon light can be seen from the village and it is understood that it's light can be seen as far away as twenty miles.

The chapel, according to the old Deeds, was approached by a pathway across the common or green. It was bounded on one side by the Bristol to Bath road and, on the other, by what is now known as Shellards Road, but at the time of its construction this was only a cart track. This road is now quite busy, and is in the process of being widened, which means that the small yard in front of the chapel will be removed and the porch will open directly onto the pavement. Approximately fifty yards from the site of the old Wesleyan chapel is another building fronting onto the main road, and which is now used as a schoolroom for the chapel. Thomas Gully for the free Methodists originally built this building in 1856. However, the owner of the adjoining property had strongly objected to the chapel being constructed in that position, and during the whole of the opening ceremony he stood in the garden at the front of his house, just to the side of the free Methodist chapel trying to disrupt the ceremony by beating a large drum.

After some while the free Methodists bought up the Wesleyan chapel property and it was enlarged to it's present size, with the old Wesleyan chapel being converted to be used as the Vestry. It is now known as a Methodist Church and is used as a place of worship, whilst the building erected by the free Methodists is now being used as a Sunday school. At the back of the Sunday school is a gallery, which was used by the choir when the building was used for Chapel services. With the idea of building a new Church, the Trustees purchased around 1900, a piece of land in front of the present Chapel, and having made the purchase, they then decided to build a boundary wall. In the minutes, which referred to this decision, it is stated that the Trustees agreed to Mr. Fry having the contract for hauling the stone and to pay him 3/6d. (£0.17½p) per horse for two horses and a man. Around the same time, the Trustees purchased the present Organ, which was being removed from the St. Philips and St. Jacobs Church, Old Market, Bristol. At a cost of £165, this was an enormous drain on the members of the Chapel and, in order to meet this price, various concerts, bazaars, jumble sales etc. were organized. At this time, the average size of the weekly collection was only six shillings (£0.30p) per week an amount that did not pay for the ordinary running expenses of the Church. To try and bridge the gap, the Sunday school scholars forfeited their prizes for several years and the cleaning of the Chapel was carried out by voluntary labour.

When the new Organ was erected, it stood in the corner of the main building, but this made it rather inconvenient for both the choir and the use of the pulpit. Accordingly it was decided to put the Organ in an Organ chamber and to rearrange the pulpit and choir stalls and, it was during these alterations, that the original doorway to the old Wesleyan chapel was found in the back wall.

Around the walls of the Sunday school are twelve pictures, painted by Mr. Watkinson, a schoolmaster of Hanham Green. They depict various incidents in the Life of Christ, and were kindly presented to the Sunday school by the artist during the latter part of the Second World War. It would seem that membership has been gradually dropping during the past years, and the number of members is now around fifty. So far the influx of new residents to the private and council estates being built nearby does not seem to have greatly affected the adult membership. There has, however, been a marked increase in the number of scholars attending Sunday school. At present, there is a caravan mission in the district, and Longwell Green is united with three other Methodist churches. Two Deaconesses are running the Mission and it is hoped to visit many of the homes on the new estate, over the months to come, in an endeavour to interest the people in Church worship.

Up to the start of the Second World War, there was a very flourishing Band of Hope, and every Whit Wednesday, there was a temperance procession with tableaux, which culminated in tea and games in a nearby field.

* * * *

In addition to the Methodists, the village could also boast the existence of a congregation representing The Mission, set up by the Plymouth Brethren, and a congregation representing The Brotherhood. During the last decade or so of the last century, representatives of the Bristol branch of the Plymouth Brethren, would frequently travel to Bitton by train and then walk around the area spreading their teaching, whilst at the same time endeavouring to convert as many of the locals as possible to their way of thinking. This they did with a modicum of success to the extent that they eventually opened a Mission in what is now the garage of a cottage on the main Bristol to Bath Road, calling their place of worship "The Welcome". This building continued to be used as a place of worship for a number of years, but in 1905, it was decided to erect a Longwell Green Mission on land adjoining Watson Road and which belonged to Dr.Short who, together with his sons were great supporters of the Mission. Mrs Short was also interested in the work of the Mission and, as his widow, still holds possession of the land. After having the necessary plans drawn up, the chapel was erected by Mr Gully at a cost of approximately £400. The chapel was dedicated towards the end of 1905, and at the opening at; least one hundred members from the sister chapel in Stokes Croft, Bristol were present.

All of the work at the Mission is carried out voluntarily, without a permanent minister. The local secretary deals with the required church business, and from time to time, a visiting preacher is engaged. Unlike the church, chapel or the brother hood, the mission draws its congregation from an area way beyond the boundaries covered by this story, particularly as it is the only place of worship of its type between Stokes Croft and Bath.

Regrettably, few records of the mission appear to be accessible and accordingly only a very general overall view can be gathered. It would seem that during the first third or so of this century, attendances were very good, despite the fact that many members had to make long journeys to and from the Mission. Understandably, with restrictions placed upon travel during the war, the levels of attendance fell away after 1939, and are only now beginning to show positive signs of getting back to their pre-war levels. The Sunday school attendance appears to have benefited from the growth of the new Council Estate, but as with other congregations, the number of adults attending services has remained fairly static.

Although started by the Plymouth Brethren, the Mission Chapel is not one of their places of worship. All the services held are very simple, without any form of choir, and when there is no visiting preacher, one of the members takes the meeting. Those who wish to be baptised into their way of believing, must undertake to be totally immersed. The Mission community still lives up to the name of their first place of worship in Longwell Green – "The Welcome".

Before leaving the subject of religious houses, it is interesting to record that despite the existence of the three separate churches/chapels, no one from the village could actually get married in any of those buildings until three years ago. Before All Saints was granted a licence, in October 1955, for marriages to be per formed in the church, all local brides had either to arrange their marriage at St.Annes, for a Church of England service, or travel to Christ Church Hanham, or Holy Trinity Kingswood. Brides with a Methodist or similar background would have to use their respective religious chapels at Oldland.

* * * * *

During 1921, meetings of the Brotherhood, which is quite independent of any of the other places of worship within Longwell Green, started to be held in the Y.M.C.A. hut, with classes every Sunday afternoon for men. Subsequently, an orchestra was formed, and as they became more proficient they would hold an open musical service on each first Sunday of the month. Within the village, the brotherhood is probably best known for the Christmas parties held each year for the children of the village. Not only did the members provide buns, cakes, trifles and all sorts of goodies, including many kinds of entertainment for the children, they also provided the older folk with tea and a small Christmas gift. Like so many traditions, life was very different after the war, and the old peoples' treat was not re-started.

It was the brotherhood that started the United Remembrance Service, now held in the church. In its heyday, there were around thirty-forty regular members, but its numbers have now dropped away, and it is only the older members who are keeping the brotherhood together.

* * * *

Along the main road towards Hanham, there stands, in its own grounds, a large stylish house, once the home of Mr.H.Budgett, provision merchant of Bristol, known as Oldland Hall which, around 1904 was acquired by the Bristol Diocesan Home for Waifs and Strays, as a gift from Admiral Close of Clifton. The home could accommodate up to thirty girls between the ages of five to sixteen and, for over twenty years there was a succession of girls who lived there, under the capable care of the matron, a Miss Humphries, who was ably assisted by Sister Kate and Sister Em. It is from the latter that we have been able to obtain much of our information concerning the daily life within the home. Our thanks accordingly go to Sister Em, now Mrs.E.Nurse, after her marriage some years ago to Charles Nurse of Olds Farm, Castle Inn Farm, Castle Road, Hanham Green, and although widowed, she still lives in the village.

During her stay at the home, Sister Em was in charge of the kitchen and the catering, whilst Sister Kate was responsible for the laundry. Together with Matron, they collectively ran the home for over twenty years with no outside help, except in the garden. When a girl reached the age of eight, she was allotted both daily and weekly chores, such as cleaning the dormitories before breakfast, cleaning boots, scrubbing the fire buckets, chopping wood etc. On most occasions, each girl would spend six or eight months perfecting each task, so that when they left school at fourteen years of age, they were trained in every sort of domestic work. The system was designed so that four girls would be allocated work in the laundry, one in the kitchen, with others learning to be dining room maids, house parlourmaids, maids to the assistant matron, whilst the position of matron's maid was always reserved for the head girl. Even though the inmates left school at fourteen, they remained at the home for a further two years, whilst they honed their skills so that, at the age of sixteen, when it was time to leave the security of the home and go out into the wide world, each girl was ready to deal with any kind of domestic work found for them.

Whilst each girl was a resident of the home she had her own savings account at the Oldland Post Office in which money could only be deposited. It was not until she left the home that the account book was given to her to be used in whatever way she thought fit.

All clothing, with the exception of hats and boots, was made in the home by members of the staff and with thirty growing girls of all shapes and sizes continuously changing, the amount of needlework undertaken by the staff must have been absolutely enormous. Each girl was provided with one navy coloured winter coat, a set of underclothes made of calico, two winter dresses, a scarf and a cardigan, and three white embroidered summer dresses, to go with their purchased white straw hats with pale blue band, with all of the material used bought from Colmers of Bath.

A typical day in the life of the home was: –

6.30am Rise and wash.
6.45am Prayers in the dormitories.
7.00am Make beds and clean dormitories.

7.45am Breakfast, followed by prayers in the Chapel.

8. 30am set off for school at St.Anne's Church of England School, a mile and a half away in Oldland.

12.30pm return to the home for the mid-day meal then walk back again to school.

4.30pm back to the home after school has ended and have a thorough wash.

5.00pm evening tea, followed by play/leisure time.

6.00pm younger children to have bath before retiring to bed.

6.30pm older children attend evening prayers in the chapel.

7.15pm older children retire to bed.

There was a playroom where their leisure time was spent, although for the older girls much of their so-called leisure time was taken up with the need for them to be knitting their own stockings. For those girls of fourteen years and over and who had already left school there was the additional responsibility to oversee the younger children, including having to see that their hair and hair ribbons were in order, and to knit the younger girl's stockings.

The girls were not allowed outside Oldland Hall on their own, particularly in the evenings, however when there were suitable social events being held in the village, they would on occasions be taken under supervision. At twelve years of age, the girls were allowed to join the Guild of St.Mary at All Saints', where they also had their own company of Girl Guides.

Each year the girls were treated to an all-day outing to Burnham-on-Sea, plus an allowance of one shilling (0.05p) each to spend how they wished. Although an apparent small amount, it should be remembered that in the years before the First World War, a shilling represented a considerable amount of money when many unskilled workers were earning less than one pound (£1) per week. In addition to this outing the young ladies would, during the month of August would very often exchange "Homes" with waifs and strays from a similar organization at Seaview, on the Isle of Wight, and occasionally with girls in other homes.

Even allowing for the above treats and obvious change in their daily routine, the girls still were able to enjoy the security and warmth of the home and the love of those in charge, with many pleasures arising from simple events and home-made pleasures, as they witnessed the many changes going on around them in the outside world, but particularly within the village itself, for example, one can only imagine at the excitement of the girls when William Bence ran his first motorbus through the village.

Excitement must have also occurred on the day it was announced that one of the girls had actually won a scholarship to Kingswood Grammar School.

Perhaps the girls' greatest excitement came with the efforts they put in to fund raising on 'Pound Day', which was an annual event held in the grounds of Oldland

Hall. In order to raise money for the upkeep of the home, this annual summer event was held with the condition that admission to the home could only be gained by visitors "paying" one pound (in weight) of any commodity at the entrance. Many people brought commodities weighing much more than, just one pound, but nevertheless, one pound of sugar or one pound of soda was sufficient to be let in. All who came must have thoroughly enjoyed themselves for in one article, printed in a local newspaper, describes a dancing display by pupils of Miss Maddocks of Bristol; an orchestra hired to play for dancing in the evening; many side shows, competitions and stalls, and bowling for children.

All the girls were required to attend All Saints' Church on Sundays, with some of the girls also being members of the choir. The vicar of St Anne's was the chaplain of the Home, but more often than not it was the curate of All Saints' who conducted a service in the girls own chapel every Friday evening. One other connection the Home had with the church was that the matron and her charges laundered the clergy's vestments, and the Communion linen, for a nominal sum, which helped to give the girls extra treats on their outings.

Every month a doctor and a dentist would visit the Home, which provided its own dentist chair, to ensure that the girl's bodies and teeth were kept healthy, and to deal with any minor ailments.

The philanthropist, Mrs.E.Jefferies who had given so much to All Saints' and the community, also donated sufficient money to the Home so that it could pay to have the stable block converted into a laundry, together with adjoining coal and wood houses. Within the laundry there were hot rollers, and a crook for heating the irons.

A member of the committee would inspect the Home each month, checking upon the general cleanliness of all parts of the building, the general well-being of the girls, the food that was being provided, and the state of the linen, and to ensure that there was no un-necessary wastage.

Overall, the majority of the girls must have been happy living in that particular community with its strict discipline and ridged routine, as many of those who left the home were prepared to meet up again in the Old Girls' Association.

The director of the Home was William Vaughan, who has recently been honoured for his lifelong service with the Church of England Children's Society.

With a certain amount of regret the Home in Longwell Green was closed on August 26th, 1930.

* * * *

EDUCATION

The earliest recollection of a school within the village itself is that of a dame's school, kept by a Mrs Tutton around 1886. It would seem that around eight or nine pupils attended the school with each paying a fee of twopence (less than one new penny) per week. They were obliged to sit on forms and irrespective of their age they were all basically taught the same standard subject by the one teacher in the one classroom, the subject being either one of the "Three R's", with just a few books provided for reading lessons. The house, which doubled as a school, still exists as one of the oldest properties in the village and is situated opposite Oldland Hall.

Beyond the village at Willsbridge, there was an earlier school, which is believed to date back to the mid 1860's. It was run by two ladies, the. Misses Stibbs, in a house now called the "Quorns". This establishment was obviously for children whose parents could afford to send them to a more select school, such as, sons and daughters of farmers, or trades people etc., with some of the children coming to the school as boarders from as far afield as Badminton. The late Rt.Rev.Armitage Robinson, D.D., Dean of Westminster, and later Dean of Wells Cathedral, received his early education at this school, whilst his father was vicar of St.John the Baptist, Keynsham. Other pupils (during the 1880's) included the children of Robert Nurse, although by this time the school was run by two other sisters, the Misses Fraser. Fanny Nurse, writing in her diary says, *"it was a long walk to the Misses Fraser's school, and I went with my friend Annie"*. Those children whose parents could not afford to send them to a private school, would walk the mile or so to either the Church of England school on Jefferies Hill, (opened 1841), or to Samuel White's Wesleyan School, which had been built around 1860.

Many years later, around 1890, the Gloucester Education Committee opened, about a mile away from the village, a new school at Cadbury Heath, appointing as its first headmaster, Henry Brain, who was then subsequently succeeded by Mr.Bodey, the father of the present headmistress of Kingswood Secondary School for Girls. The building of the new school at Cadbury Heath was designed to have Longwell Green in its catchment's area, and accordingly many children from the village now began to make their way to the new school, and this arrangement continues right up to the present time. In 1910, a new school, The Meadows, was opened in Bitton, some two miles away from the village, and as this meant that few, if any, of the Longwell Green children would use this new educational facility, the rate-payers of the village objected most strongly to having to contribute to the cost of the new school. In general they felt that the three schools already in existence were adequate for the needs of the village children. With the passage of time emotions have changed, and now, and for many years past, quite a number of village children have attended The Meadows, despite the greater distance.

With an ever-increasing population in the expanding village, the above schools have been found to be inadequate to meet the demand, so that around 1935, another school, Hanham Abbots Primary, was constructed. However, since the war, there has been the influx of Bristol overspill families to cater for and accordingly, there has, during the past four years, been the construction of a large primary school on the housing estate, built on the fringe of Longwell Green. Thus there is now quite a wide choice of schools for the children of the village and the surrounding area to attend. In the old days the siting of a school away from the village, very often lead to extra cost being incurred with regard to the children's footwear, whereas nowadays the cost is in bus fares. Nevertheless, the education authorities over the years have not deemed it necessary, probably in view of the small number of children involved, to provide a school in the village itself.

* * * *

Adult evening classes and lectures have been held in Longwell Green since the turn of the century, with the first known reference being in the Parish Council October 1901 minutes, which records: –

Mr.Robert Francis Nurse was elected to serve on the local committee formed to deal with the technical instruction committee of the Gloucester County Council, Southern Centre.

In April 1905, ambulance classes for men were started followed, some seventeen months later, by a request for a sick-nursing class for women. Miss Higgins, of Willsbridge House, was asked to form a ladies' committee to advertise and manage this course. Gardening classes followed in April 1909, with all three well attended and supported, in fact the sick nursing class had an average attendance of twenty-six women over the whole time it was in existence. From the ambulance class, Mr.A.Nurse gained a silver medallion for the level of skill obtained. In September 1914 a cookery class started with the help of the County Council who provided all of the necessary equipment. Although not as numerically successful as the sick nursing class, the average number of students still stood at; fifteen. Later as the war on the continent ground to a stalemate, lectures were held upon the keeping of poultry, which also proved to be a great success. These well-tried and favourite classes continued for over thirty years, and it was not until 1938 that a new subject was added to the curriculum. As the shadow of the war clouds spread its fear and concern over the land, especially the potential threat of many civilian casualties as a result of terror bombing, it was suggested that lectures should be given on the subject of air-raid precaution. Accordingly, in April 1938, a list of names of those prepared to offer their services to the newly formed A.R.P. was made, and classes were arranged for those persons to attend. At first, the lectures/instructions concentrated upon the very real and worrying threat of gas attacks and the required anti-gas precautions. Many of those who were in the Council and who sat on A.RP. Committees were old enough to remember quite vividly the terrible effects gas had had during the First World War on men in the trenches, and of course there were some men in the community who were still suffering from having been gassed during those hostilities. Once this subject was instilled into the minds of the volunteers, the scope of the lectures widened to cover many other possible aspects of aerial warfare.

Not unexpectedly, the war years took its toll on the classes held and as a consequence the majority were postponed for the duration. However as the memory of the war began to subside, so attention was given to the re-opening of evening classes, and by 1948 the Gloucestershire Education Committee had begun to sponsor classes involving dressmaking; embroidery; handicrafts, and drama. Gardening classes came under the auspices of the Hartbury Farm Institute of Gloucester, whilst a lecturer, provided by the University of Bristol, held two sessions of Musical Appreciation, and extra mural studies. The interest in these subjects originated from members of the Women's Institute, and is fostered by the Longwell Green Memorial and Playing Fields Association.

* * * *

For many years there had been a huge desire for the village to have it's own library and, after many months of pressure on the County Council they eventually agreed to open a library in the Y.M.C.A. hut on March 14th, 1929. At the beginning, Mr.Alfred Lovell offered his services as the librarian, and started with a collection of three hundred books, and twenty members. The books were housed on shelves made by members of the Y.M.C.A. and donated to the library fee of charge. Although the collection of books now in circulation has grown to just over one thousand, and the membership to two hundred and sixty-three, the library still operates from the same premises. One other fact of great importance is that the librarianship has remained in the same Lovell family as it started, with daughters following in father's footsteps, and all in a purely honorary capacity.

* * * *

Members of the Comic Cricket Match held in the village c1953

Anyone for tennis c1953

The 1948 Fancy Dress procession stops in Shellards Road to have their picture taken.

Villagers at the Annual Supper. March 1950

Members of the Brotherhood Orchestra 1930

Member and officials of the Willsbridge Amateur Football Club 1911

A young lady sits sidesaddle on her donkey near Kingsfield lane c1895

The International voluntary workers organised by the Society of Friends at the Community Centre stone laying ceremony August 1956

SOCIAL ACTIVITIES

The social activities of the village can be divided into three distinct periods of time, being the period before the First World War; the period between both wars, and from the end of the Second World War to the present day.

During the first period, the social activities were centred on the Church, the Chapel and the two village inns. *The Wheatsheaf* and *The Crown*. In 1896, a tin church was erected in the village, and on the land behind which had been purchased and given to the village by Henry Fry, a hut was built. This hut soon became a mecca for all kinds of social events to be held in the village, including dances, dancing classes, socials, whist drives, concerts and other such functions. Concerts were very often performed by local talent of varying degree and skill, but one of the most popular shows was "Mrs.Jarley's Waxworks", in which an historical, dramatic, or picturesque tableau was staged, using local residents as the motionless models.

Whist drives during this period were very well attended, with prizes being supplied by the village benefactor, Mrs Jefferies who, throughout her lifetime, never failed in her enormous interest in the village and its people.

With regard to outdoor activities, there was a football team, which was run under the encouragement of the Chapel, who used to play in a field at the top of Gully's Lime Quarry, in what was then called Lime Kiln Lane, but of course is now known as Court Farm Road. The team continued to use that particular field for twelve or more years prior to the First World War, the only problem they had was, that at the end of each playing season, the edge of the quarry was becoming nearer and nearer to the pitch as the quarrying activities were expanded. In due course the field as a football pitch had to close as too many balls were being lost over the edge, and it would have been too dangerous to have continue playing competitive games on the edge of such a drop.

After the war to end all wars had stopped its desolation, and the survivors returned home, it was felt that there was a need to re-build a. football team to represent the village. However, the only person prepared to make the necessary arrangements was the landlord of *The Wheatsheaf Inn* who set about organising and running a team who had their home pitch at the rear of the inn. In addition those men who had returned from the mud of Flanders and who had experienced a great deal of comradeship within their units and in the trenches, wanted some kind of club, where they could go and relax amongst their fellow men. Accordingly the Young Men's Christian Association was approached to see if they would open one of their branches in Longwell Green. The Y.M.C.A. had a number of war-surplus huts scattered around, the county, one of which was then standing at Patchway and it was this one that was offered to the village, provided it was taken down and re-erected without any cost to the Association. Having then obtained the appropriate permission from the Chapel Trustees, the hut was dismantled, by Messrs James

Gully & Sons, brought to Longwell Green and re-erected on land belonging to the chapel, where it remains to this day. Having a hut was one thing but on its own it was just an empty space, and accordingly the question of furnishings was the next problem on the agenda. Soon the embryonic club had received an offer of a billiard table, chairs and tables, all of which needed to be collected from Amesbury and, with much support for the whole project, it was not long before a very flourishing club came into being. Not content to sit indoors on all occasions, particularly during the summer months, they succeeded in persuading Mr.Fusell, who was himself very interested in the club, to allow them the use one of his fields, free of charge, so that they could lay out a cricket pitch, and three tennis courts. Eventually, after much hard work in preparing the ground, the club were able to boast of these extra summer attractions, which were also well patronized. These extra activities were in addition, an excellent vehicle for raising funds, which in turn meant that by the end of the first season, the club were able to hand over a considerable sum of money to the Y.M.C.A. In June of each year, the village held a carnival, when around forty or fifty people took part, wearing fancy dress and, having paraded around the "triangle", the participants were all invited to a strawberry tea, followed by races, in which both children and adults took part, although of course not at the same time. One major feature of the day, which caused a lot of excitement and anticipation, was the arrival of the "Pocket Lady". This was one of the lady helpers, who wore a crinoline dress made of patchwork, with hoops and a hundred or so pockets in the skirt. The pockets were numbered, and were offered for sale at three pence each, with just some of the pockets containing a lucky prize winning number.

Variety concerts were held at regular intervals, with an admission charge of sixpence (0.2½p) for adults, and half price for children.

After the Second World War it was felt that a Hall, in memory of those who had fallen during the conflict, should be erected in the village, and during the autumn of 1945 an exploratory committee was set up which resulted in the formation of the Longwell Green War Memorial & Playing Fields Association in March 1946. Land in Shellards Road was purchased, and various committees, such as planning, membership, building etc., were formed. In addition other organisations were approached and co-opted on to committees, which soon contained representatives from the British Legion, Parish Councils, plus both the church and the chapel. The membership now totalled around four hundred, and various functions were held to raise the funds needed to start the construction of the hall.

A number of years were to pass before sufficient funds had been collected together to start the building, with the first turf not being cut until August 1955 All of those involved with the construction were volunteers, who toiled throughout the remainder of that year and well in to the following year. In August of 1956, a work camp was organised by the Society of Friends, so that members of the camp, who represented about eleven different nationalities, could help with the basic groundwork and initial building. During their time in the village they camped either in tents in the field, or used existing halls in which to sleep. Very good progress was made with the work by these visitors from overseas and by the local volunteers, and the whole exercise brought extra life to the village, providing fun for the younger members of society, and giving the older ones an opportunity to entertain the visitors English style. A dance and a barbecue were held, and it proved to be a very happy and successful month for all concerned.

It was on the 18th August 1956 that Alderman Henry Crook, laid the Foundation Stone, when a short service was held, during which time various other organisations involved with the initial development of the project were also invited to lay bricks. At the present time the work of building is still in progress by a small, but very enthusiastic and dedicated, band of workers, who attend on site whenever possible, and who hope to have the building completed in the near future. After such a long time, there are many in the village that await this event with eager anticipation.

There are a number of outdoor sports events connected with this organisation including, members of the thriving tennis club, who are very grateful to be able to meet and play on a court kindly loaned to them by Mrs.Bull. In addition there is a ladies' hockey team, and it is hoped that in the not too distant future, football and cricket teams will also be formed.

In the past a number of Flower Shows used to be held, but over more recent years the popularity of such shows has waned, and now they have been totally discontinued.

Some four years ago, it was felt by many ladies living in the area, that a Women's Institute should be formed, and after corresponding with the Gloucestershire Federation, sanction was granted, and now the Institute is one of the leading social activities in the village.

There have, during the first half of this century, been a number of Official Celebrations held in and around the village, recalled as under: –

1902 Coronation of Edward VII:

To celebrate this event, a single row of plane trees was planted along one side of the main road, together with a solitary oak tree planted just outside the church. As we can see today, the plane trees have flourished and grown, but sadly the oak died.

1935 King George V Jubilee:

On this occasion twelve hundred people from both parishes were entertained to tea, and a fête was held in a field in the parish of Oldland. A tea and concert was arranged for the old folk, and for those who were unfortunately incapacitated, a small gift was provided.

1937 Coronation of George VI:

A tea party was held for the children in the area, with gifts of sweets and a Coronation mug to take home. For members of the older generation, gifts of tea and tobacco were provided, but as a more permanent celebration, a six and a half acre playing field in the parish of Oldland, was dedicated.

1951 Festival of Britain:

Wayside seats were dedicated in the parish of Oldland by Anthony Crosland M.P. ably assisted by the Rev.E.H.Patey, vicar of St.Anne's, Oldland, with All Saints' Longwell Green.

1953 Coronation of Queen Elizabeth II:

Two oak trees were planted by school children at Parkwall, in the parish of Oldland, on the new Bristol overspill estate, now springing up adjacent to the village. Wayside seats were dedicated in the Hanham Abbots parish, one of which was situated at the top of Willsbridge Hill, near to "Northfield", with the other located at, Hanham Green. A celebratory mug was given to every child in both parishes.

New and improved technology in the world of communication meant that this would be the first Coronation to be televised to the nation at large. Whilst few families in and around Longwell Green owned a TV set, it was possible to bring a television receiver in to the Church Hall and invite the old folk to watch the spectacle live on the small screen. At the same time a fête and fancy dress parade was organised.

As a general celebration, a fund for all parishioners over the age of sixty-five is organised so that each year they can receive a parcel of groceries.

* * * *

So ends the story of Longwell Green during the past one hundred years. Not perhaps, an outstanding one, or one of great historical or architectural interest, but to its inhabitants, and especially to the members of the Women's Institute, it really is "OUR VILLAGE"

As a tribute to the Members of the Women's Institute this picture c1961 of the Longwell Green group is reproduced by kind permission of Mrs.Christine Parnell

SECTION 2

A PHOTOGRAPHIC LOOK BACK

AT OUR VILLAGE

AND THE

SURROUNDING AREA

Compiled August 2001

The Following section of this book enables the reader to take an armchair journey back in time with a study of old photographs taken from the Author's collection of the area covered by the written story as set out in Section 1. This visual story starts from where my highly recommended book *"AROUND BITTON"* ends and, in conjunction with the old favourite *"BITTON (EAST) THEN & NOW"* gives all those who are interested a complete and fascinating early twentieth century pictorial record of the original main road between Bristol and Bath, covering the area from the Hanham border through to and including Kelston.

POST OFFICE WILLSBRIDGE. 14.

The upper part of Willsbridge showing the Post Office, with postmistress and dog outside. Both the pedestrian and the local delivery man have been asked to stand still whilst the photograph is taken, note Bitton Station in background. c1904.

WILLSBRIDGE.

The lower section of Willsbridge village looking down from Brockham Hill, as the main road sweeps through and on up the hill past Willsbridge House. c1906.

Where Brockham Hill meets Willsbridge Hill, showing part of an old cottage on the right, and a glimpse of the *Queen's Head* on the left. c1905.

A very similar but older view showing more of the ivy covered "Castle" and more of the roadway which appears to be in a very muddy condition. c1901.

The Mill Pond showing heavy vegetation and calm water waiting to be sent through the mill chase where its power will turn the large wheel. c1913.

The front of the Mill with water pouring over the sluice gates on the left. Note the triangular shaped Dovecote halfway up the main building, c1905

CATSCLIFF,
WILLSBRIDGE

A. R. Bence.
P.O., Willsbridge

The summer sunshine filters through the leafy glade at Catscliffe.

Looking back towards the bend in Willsbridge Hill, with *The Limes* in the centre background, and the main entrance to Willsbridge House on the right.

Having survived for many years as an elegant and well-built family home, these pictures show Oldbury Chase having been under attack from Travellers, who broke into the disused property and systematically set about destroying as much as they could. Fortunately there was enough of the exterior of the building left when these pictures were taken to show how splendid the house was. 28 August 1986.

Although the quality of the photograph is not that good as it is one of the very few pictures looking back down from the top of the hill it needed to be included. c1902

The view from Willsbridge House showing the cluster of properties in Willsbridge Bottom, and the group at the junction of the Bath road with the Keynsham Road. Beyond the most southerly slopes of the Cotswolds can be seen.

Top of Willsbridge Hill. 826.

The top of Willsbridge Hill towards Longwell Green, with Court Farm Road off to the left. A busy junction today but, when this picture was taken the only wheeled vehicle in sight were the little boy on a tricycle, and a single deck bus coming around the corner. c1930.

The entrance to Oliver Keeling & Sons', limekilns in Stouts Hill, (now Court Farm Road) with a posed picture of staff and carriers. c1910.

In the grounds of Harefield Hall

The main road as it sweeps around towards the centre of the village, with neat clipped trees on the right. Just one cyclist, four cars and one bus occupy the otherwise deserted road. c1936

Close up view of *The Wheatsheaf Inn* together with the landlord, landlady, and a group of their customers. Although the inn has long since closed, the building still remains. c1910.

LONGWELL GREEN VILLAGE.

These two pictures are of the same area but eighty years apart in time. Above can be seen the newly planted Coronation Trees, with the Tin Church behind, in contrast to the maturity of those trees below, and other changes which have taken place over the years. The lower picture was taken on the 8 August 1987, whilst the above picture is dated around 1908

Above, the villagers go about their business, or gather to chitchat in the warm summer sunshine, whilst below winter has stripped the leaves off the trees. The tin church can be clearly seen with All Saints' just visible in the lower picture, both of which were taken around 1911

Outside the *Crown Hotel* young ladies and very ornate perambulators stand with the village postman to await the photographer's instructions. Only the little girl by the water trough fails to look at the camera. c1906.

By the time that this picture was taken, some twenty years later, the *Crown Inn* has been partially re-built and is no longer a hotel. The ladies dress style has changed, and motorcars make use of the new garage almost hidden behind the trees. c1927.

A group of people stand outside Pomeroy's shop, next to the local garage selling Mex petrol (still independent of Shell). The Shellards Road turning can be seen to the left of the cyclist. c1927

Around 1907, young children play outside the tin church, whilst a young lady in her summer refinery strolls along in the sunshine. Glentworth House advertises millinery, drapery and hosiery. It will be many years before Ellacombe Road is built.

An exterior and interior shot of All Saints' Church, with the former taken from a card posted in 1911 with the comment: "Dear Nell, what do you think of our new church?", whilst on the back of the second card, the message reads: "This is a rather good photo. of the interior of our church. Of course it is still very bare we have only the shell yet, but some day I hope it will be magnificent, none in the district to compare with". Both cards c1910.

Two pictures showing the approach and full frontage of Oldland Hall, taken not long after it had become the Diocesan Home for waifs and strays c1905

Bristol Diocesan Home. "Recreation".

Part of a small series of cards showing the internal activities of the Diocesan Home, with above, Sisters Em and Kate with the children at play, and below the same Sisters and Matron Humphries at the meal table.c1904

Bristol Diocesan Home. "Dinnertime".

Bristol Diocesan Home. "Busy as Bees".

Above Sister Kate teaching the young girls needlework and laundry work, whilst below is one of the dormitories for the under twelve's. c1904.

Bristol Diocesan Home. "Bedtime."

The 1925 Guild outing to Bournemouth is about to start, with the Sunday school teachers seated in the middle of the charabanc. The message on the card includes "the remainder are Guild, see our substantial Matron"!!.

Court Farm Road (Stouts Hill) looking towards the junction of Bath Road with Willsbridge Hill.c1903

The 'very recognizable "Sally-on-the-Barn" taken at a time when a variety of animals were kept, including carthorses used both on the farm and to take away the farm produce and to return with supplies. This picture has been carefully orchestrated by the photographer, to give an atmosphere of life as it was almost one hundred years ago. c1905.

Old cottages about to be pulled down to allow for the expansion of the Shell filling
station facing Bath Road. 31 March 1989.

A close-up picture, showing the front of All Saints' Church c1950. Reproduced by
kind permission of Kenneth Meek

Longwell Green Constabulary raised to deal with wartime civilian duties. Top row l/r. Special Constables Jones, Jenkins and Darby, (the latter being the butcher from Oldland). Seated l/r. Special Constable Caswell, Constable Gilbert Meek (officer in charge), and Special Constable Lewis. c1940. By kind permission of Kenneth Meek.

A cottage, in Pound Lane, the day after it had been hit by lightening during the terrific storm of 4 July 1915.

Recently constructed houses in Shellards Road showing Mr. Musty working on the stretch of unmade footpath. The car is close to the junction with Pit Lane, whilst in the fields now occupied by a housing estate, stands two large haystacks. c1938.

California Road after the sale of California Farm for building purposes. The road has been widened and work is about to start on the construction of the new private housing estate. c1980.

PARKWALL VILLA F.C.

1924–25

| BILL HARDING | BILL PERROT | CLIFF LONG | ELLIS SHORT | HAROLD HARDING | FRED STONE | FARMER COUSINS |

| PERCY ADAMS | BILL HANKS | CHARLES HARVEY | WALLY HANKS | CHARLIE PLUMPTON | FRED WOOD |

| BILL POMEROY | RON SIMS | ALBERT WILLIAMS | TOM JENNINGS | SAM LONG |

HOME GROUND WAS ON WHAT IS NOW 'EARLSTONE CRESCENT'

Parkwall Villa F.C. 1924-25.

Mr. Hallett; cutting wheat on Mr. Davis's farm some where on the Parkwall Estate, and possibly near to, or part, of today's Parkwall County Primary School. c1950.

Girls of Cadbury Heath School 1920.

Transport of yesteryear, with above Norman Hall proudly showing off his new delivery van and gold medal cup for his washing compound "EEZALL".c1908. Below Mr.C.Fry shows his son the controls of his new "peoples carrier" with his military style driver making sure that nothing goes wrong with his charge. c1927.

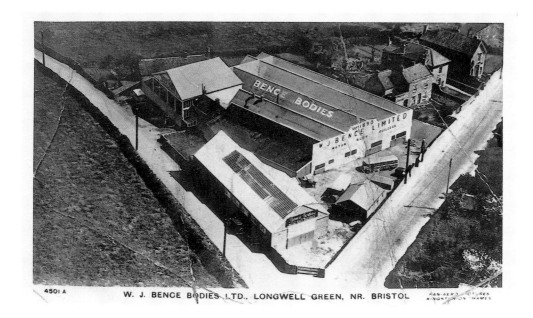

An aerial view of W.J.Bence Ltd works with single deck bus in yard, and cottages and large house behind. c1922. Below an empty Stone Hill (Bath Road) looking back towards Longwell Green. c1930.

Cottages, adjacent to W.J. Bence Ltd, facing Bath Road (see previous aerial photograph). c1957. Reproduced by kind permission of David G. Elliott.

These cottages which face Kingsfield Lane are behind the coachworks, .
Reproduced by kind permission of David G. Elliott.

Stonehill looking towards Warmley prior to the construction of Avon Ring Road, and the development of the leisure complex, showing the Allied Carpets Warehouse built in the 1980's and pulled down in the 1990's to be replaced by Comet and B&Q Superstores. December 1991.

Two different views of Longwell Green Poultry Farm, which was situated at Stonehill not far from the present bridge over the Avon Ring Road. c1910.

The junction of Castle Farm Road with Water Lane, showing a small cluster of attractive properties including the Castle Inn. c1908

Although the definition of the picture is not that good, its historical importance required the inclusion of this picture of the cottages and their inhabitants at Hanham Mills c1908

NEAR HANHAM LOCK 655.

The above, is a much-improved picture of the same cottages, but there are no inhabitants to add to the interest and composition. Note the additional improvements of guttering and internal drainage. c1930. Below is an even older view of the same area looking in the opposite direction when the cottages were covered in ivy. c1903

Looking along the riverbank towards the *Old Chequers Inn* with a horse and cart passing by, and small group negotiating the price of hiring a rowing boat. c 1907. Below local river men wait for their next job, whilst behind can be seen the quarrying scars and the cottage gardens as they sweep down to the waters edge. C1903

Above: the barges *Blanche* and *George* are at rest in a quiet backwater of Hanham; taken from a post-card used as a birthday card on the 24 February 1905. Below: a view of the river at Hanham Mills as its sweeps around to the right through the Somerdale meadows, with St.John the Baptist church tower at Keynsham in the background. c1924

Cows graze in the field unconcerned that the bargeman is struggling to keep his
barge heading down stream towards Bristol. Another barge appears to be stationary
whilst both the horses and their minders wait patiently on the towpath. c1920.
Below: Hanham Ferry from the Somerset side, with ferry just pulling away from
the opposite bank. c1906

Hanham Ferry Nr Bristol. 141.

The river lock at Hanham Mills. c1910

Part of Hanham Woods above, whilst below Mr. Ellis, of Hall Farm, is gathering a
very good crop of mangel-wurzels. c1912.

Two exterior shots of Hanham Court showing in the above view the well manicured lawn, both wings and connecting turret from the back, whilst below is the view of the Court and adjoining church from the front. Note old barn on right. Both pictures taken around 1905.

The lofty oak-panelled Dining Room, of Hanham Court with ornate sideboard, and family portraits c1920.

SECTION 3

LONGWELL GREEN COACHWORKS

And

BENCE MOTOR SERVICES

A STORY OF

W.J.BENCE & SONS

AUGUST 2001

Sometime during the early 1890's, the local wheelwright and entrepreneur William (Bill) J. Bence began operating a horse-drawn carrier business, connecting villages such as Doynton; Oldland; Bitton; Warmley; Longwell Green, and Hanham with Bristol. Although primarily set up for the carriage of goods, especially on market days, Mr. Bence actively encouraged the conveyance of passengers between the various villages and the heart of Bristol, usually terminating at the *White Hart* Old Market Street. Regrettably there are no surviving records of the number of passengers carried in this way during the last decade of the nineteenth century, all that can be determined is that with the *White Hart* being used by around fourteen or fifteen other carriers, and with Old Market Street being developed during the mid 1890's as the terminus of the Bristol Tramway & Carriage Company's new electric car service to Kingswood, and subsequently Eastville, Old Market Street must have been a very congested road indeed.

Nevertheless, even without any records, circumstances would seem to indicate that those who lived out in the country and who wished to travel into and out of the city found Mr. Bence's carts very convenient, if sometimes the only means of conveyance. However despite the success he was enjoying, Bill's main interest and traditional skill was as a wheelwright, but not at the expense of progress. Fortunately, William (Bill) was slightly different to his fellow men, particularly those who rejected changes and stuck to old fashion traditions, inasmuch as he had the courage and the foresight to see that the new twentieth century was going to hold many changes which would effect all citizens and which needed to be grasped with both hands if his ambition to become a successful wealthy business man was to be realized. For hundreds of years, wheelwrights had been skilled in the art of working with wood, and did not just stick solely to making wheels but instead, they would more often than not, build the whole coach, cart or wagon, themselves. William was no exception to this rule, and actively built up his business as a quality coach builder and wheelwright in premises owned by him which faced onto Stonehill, at its junction with Kingsfield Lane.

During the fifteen or so years from 1890, his business ventures grew and grew, so that around 1905/08, he made his sons Henry and Albert partners in the business, re-titled, W.J.BENCE & SONS.

Ever the entrepreneur and man of foresight, William enthused about the very obvious changes that were being made in transport, and in particular the transportation of the masses, especially following the huge growth of the railways. Now as the new century unfolded, there was a new fangled internal combustion engine to contend with, which William felt certain was going to revolutionize future road transport.

Like most new inventions the development of the motor car, the motor bus and the motor lorry moved quite slowly, and few had the wealth to enjoy the thrill of riding a motorized vehicle, and in the backwaters of south Gloucestershire matters moved at an even slower pace. Accordingly William and his sons had to control their enthusiasm, and concentrate instead on the promotion and well-being of their coach building, wheelwright and carrier businesses and whilst Britain remained at the head of a great Empire, and her navy ruled the waves, nearly all who lived in the country during the early part of the last century, were able to get on with their lives to varying degrees, safe in the knowledge that their country was safe and secure. Unfortunately things were about to change but not in the way that William wanted as a challenge was made to Britain's supremacy, and a war in Europe started in 1914.

One of the things that so often happen when a country goes to war is that the promotion and development of inventions increases, and by the end of the conflict, mechanical lorries and buses had become quite a common place, which gave William and his sons the opportunity they required.

As far as can be determined, the horse-drawn carrier business run by the Bence family continued through to around 1918. However, by then it was possible to obtain, at quite a reasonable price, second-hand lorries, and it seem most likely that two or three such vehicles were acquired by W.J.Bence & Sons, as they inaugurated a motorized transport business during that year. In addition, in conjunction with one of William's daughters, and Mabel Gough, daughter of the landlord of the *Butcher's Arms* they helped set up a car hire business. By the end of 1918, and on into the following year, the firm began to purchase ex War Department Daimler bus chassis, and fitted them with a single-deck bus body in their own workshop. This then enabled the firm to commence operating a motorized bus service during 1919. By the following year, a stage carriage service had started between Hanham and Kingswood via Warmley; Oldland and Longwell Green, with extra routes to Bitton. Keynsham, Downend and Staple Hill, being developed over the following few years.

The very first drivers to be appointed by Mr. Bence were Albert (Bert) Morgan, and Ernest Webb, who lived in Shellards Road and it was Ernest who was asked to drive one of the 14-seater buses on a test run to verify the timings for the proposed timetable. Many years later he recalled how he drove one of the buses, with the bodywork by Bence, on a Ford Chassis, out of the Hanham bus depot, and set off, on solid rear tyres, along the country roads leading to Longwell Green, then on to Willsbridge, left up Cherry Garden Hill to Oldland Common, left at the Union Inn, over the railway and down Cowhorn Hill, then along Tower Road North and South to Warmley and up the hill to Kingswood, finishing the route at the tram terminus. At all stages of the journey he needed to note the time taken so that appropriate fare stages could be settled with arrival/setting off times, and so well did he carry out this work that it is said that the service ran like clockwork, with the buses always running to time, so much so that their reliability was remembered by all who lived in the area.

The early days of the partnership with above, a farm-cart newly built for Edward Brie of Park Farm, at the factory entrance, as is also, in the picture below, a flat bed cart for Henry J. Fry & Sons of Willsbridge, c1907.

William Bence with his sons around him, and his faithful dog and constant companion, "Spot" keeping a close watch on the photographer as he records the completion of their farm wagon for Arthur Ford of Cardiff. c1908.

William Bence stands behind on of the in-house flat bed carts built for company use with his workforce outside the turning shed. c1906.

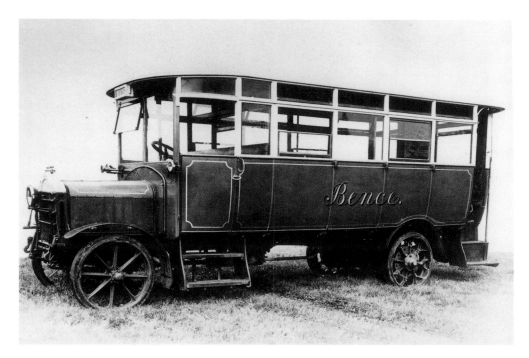

Newly out-shopped, a brand new bodied bus on a Daimler chassis, and four solid tyres, about to go into service for Mr, Bence under his fleet number 15. Note door of the left which would allow two or three passengers the right to sit up with the driver, c1919. Below: AE 2782 with driver, conductor and friends, stand outside the *White Hart,* the Bitton terminus of route 36 to Hanham via Oldland. c1919.

Over the next few years the little 14-seater buses in the green and white livery of Bence's Bus Service, became a very familiar sight around Hanham, Longwell Green, Bitton, Oldland, Keynsham, Bridgeyate, Kingswood and Staple Hill. Not only was it their reliability which made the service so popular, it was also the little personal touches of drivers who kept a friendly eye open for late passengers hurrying through the garden gate or along the lane to the bus stop. Then there was the driver who would stop outside a passenger's house, particularly when it was raining, to save the customer from having to walk back from the bus stop. When Ernest Webb was on duty in the area of his home, there were times when driving through Shellards Road could be something of a hazard due to everyone knowing him and the phrase "personal service" had a special meaning of its own as he could be called upon to pick up, or drop off passengers on as many as six separate occasions and still find himself and the bus in Shellards Road. With a cheery countenance, Ernest would happily perform these extra duties and still ensure that his bus ran to time.

Of course it was not only the drivers who helped promote the friendliness of the service, it was also the conductors, such as Reg Blake, Fred Gardner and Alfred Nicholls, all from Hanham, who met and greeted their passengers with a gleeful hello. In the early days, the conductors had no ticket holder or punch machine, and more often than not, they were seen with the rolls of tickets hung around their neck, which were issued to each passenger after having been torn from the perforated roll, and then clipped for cancellation. Originally there were no bells to ring, instead the conductors were supplied with whistles, which at times could be quite deafening to any passenger close to the blast, especially on those occasions when the crew had allowed many more passengers onboard than the stipulated 14. Quite often there would be ten or twelve people standing, and it is reputed that on at least one occasion the little 14-seater bus was carrying an extra thirty passengers but, how well, or perhaps how poorly, the bus coped with the many hills on route has not been recorded.

The early buses had solid back tyres, with pneumatic front tyres, which must have produced a rather strange motion as the bus travelled the country roads, especially as these buses also had a rather fierce clutch which could easily send the unwary driver and his charge shuddering along the road for a moment or two, as he tried to pull away from the stop. He, of course, was sat down and holding onto a steering wheel, but that was not always true of all of his passengers, who in their stoical way, appeared to take the odd knock in their stride, even when the spasmodic movement of the bus sent them sprawling to the floor.

The buses were also fitted with oil side lamps, which had the extremely irritating and potentially dangerous habit of blowing out on windy nights leading, on one or two occasions when it was particularly stormy, to the intrepid conductor having to sit astride the bonnet with a battery powered cycle lamp in each extended hand to warn other road users that the bus was on its way. Although highly illegal under the Road

Traffic Act, and also highly dangerous for the adventurous conductor, the arrangement presumably meant that the passengers reached their destination, even though the driver, with his conductor sat in front of him, was no doubt able to guess, if not see, which way he was going. How fortuitous that there were many less vehicles on the roads then, than there are today.

As the services grew and as more and more route miles were being driven, and more passengers being carried, the number of buses required also increased, which lead to the firm buying five or six Ford chassis on which 14-seat Bence bodies were constructed, plus the acquisition of three of four Napier charabancs which were then converted into buses.

By 1923, the business partnership between William and his sons had grown quite considerably, and it was decided by the family to convert the business into a limited company thus, it was during this year that W.J.Bence Ltd was created. For the next seven years this local friendly and well-patronized business continued to flourish, particularly with the help of the loyal locals who almost felt that the bus company was part of the family. However the expansion of the bus service was being compromised by the expansion, into their territory, of the much larger Bristol Tramway & Carriage Co Ltd. As the big fish eyed the small fish, talks inevitably started on a possible take-over, and in March 1930 the larger company took over the family business, but allowed the local name to remain by forming a new company to be known as Bence Motor Services Ltd. William and his sons were given shares in this new company, and it is believed that they were all appointed Directors, although this privilege may have only extended to William. In addition the new company was also provided with buses supplied by the BTCC.

For the next five years this "shot-gun marriage" appears to have worked but like most enforced marriages, particularly where one of the partners is much more dominant than the other, the relationship was not always a comfortable one. Sadly, during 1935, the entrepreneur William J.Bence died, and with him went the need for autonomy within Bence Motor Services Ltd. Having then allowed a reasonable time for mourning, the Bristol Tramway & Carriage Co Ltd., in June 1936, completely absorbed the local business, and the name Bence no longer existed as far as a bus company was concerned.

In addition to operating a bus company, William Bence had also built up a fleet of coaches under the name "Queen of the West", and this part of the business, together with the bus garage and filling station at Hanham, were at the same time also absorbed into the BTCC.

However, this was not the end of the Bence business only a curtailment, and left in the hands of the family was the filling station at Willsbridge, and the coachworks at Longwell Green. It was earlier mentioned that in 1918 the original part of William's business had started to build bus and lorry bodies for its own business, and this side

One of the Ford 'T' model 14-seat bus believed to be at the Staple Hill terminus during its inaugural journey on the Hanham-Downend route, with Driver Ernest Webb, and his conductor Fred Gardner. c1922. From the Peter Davey British Omnibus Photograph Collection.

Hanham and Downend Service

FARES.

FROM \ TO	Hanham	Terra Cotta	Kingswood	Star	Staple Hill	Downend
HANHAM		1d.	1½d.	2½d.	3d.	4d.
Terra Cotta	1d.		1d.	2d.	2½d.	3½d.
Kingswood (Downend Road)	1½d.	1d.		1d.	1½d.	2½d.
Star, Soundwell	2½d.	2d.	1d.		1d.	2d.
Staple Hill (Porteullis)	3d.	2½d.	1½d.	1d.		1d.
DOWNEND	4d.	3½d.	2½d.	2d.	1d.	

Children under 3 years—Free; 3 to 12 years—Half Ordinary Fares. Any Fraction of ½d. counted as ½d.

Hanham and Downend Service

Sundays.

	p.m.	p.m.	p.m.	p.m.	And every 15 minutes until	p.m.
HANHAM ... dep.	1.15	1.30	1.45	2.0		10.15
Terra Cotta	1.22	1.37	1.52	2.7		10.22
Kingswood (Hall's Rd.)	1.27	1.42	1.57	2.12		10.27
Star, Soundwell	1.32	1.47	2.2	2.17		10.32
Staple Hill (Porteullis)	1.35	1.50	2.5	2.20		10.35
DOWNEND ... arr.	1.37	1.52	2.7	2.22		10.37
DOWNEND ... dep.	1.38	1.53	2.8	2.23		10.38
Staple Hill (Porteullis)	1.40	1.55	2.10	2.25		10.40
Star, Soundwell	1.43	1.58	2.13	2.28		10.43
Kingswood (Downend Rd.)	1.48	2.3	2.18	2.33		10.48
Terra Cotta	1.53	2.8	2.23	2.38		10.53
HANHAM ... arr.	2.0	2.15	2.30	2.45		11.0

Advertising the quality of their workmanship, as a new delivery van built for
J.W.Long of Staple Hill stands outside of the workshop at Longwell Green in all
of its glory with Spot at the controls. c1914. Below a number of the company's
buses and their crew are lined up outside Bence Garage Longwell Green c1924.

A rear-end view of the newly out-shopped Daimler No.15 as it is posed in the field adjoining the factory. c1919. Below Albion bus No 20 is positioned amongst the houses on a bright summers day during the early 1930's.

of the Bence empire had also continued to grow, and develop through the 1920's. Not only did it supply the Bence fleet, it also built bus bodies that were operated throughout the Southwest and South Wales, plus three buses that were purchased by a small coach company in Manchester. By 1929 a distributorship had been taken up with an associated company of Guy Motors, and a number of coaches built to the "Star Flyer" design were constructed at Longwell Green.

From around 1925, Bence had built a number of bodies on chassis supplied by the Canadian Reo Company, (of Fire-engine fame) both for Reo's own use and the use of some of Bence's customers. However this work was carried out at the expense of the Bristol based company Harris & Hassel Ltd., and having lost the original contract, this company decided to produce their own vehicles, with many of them (possibly up to 70-80) being bodied by Bence. Although this was an extremely useful contract for Bence it only lasted about five years as in 1930, Harris & Hassel Ltd, were placed in voluntary liquidation.

Fortunately, throughout the whole of this decade, a greater number of goods vehicle bodies were also being supplied by W.J.Bence Ltd., as these, in the main, tended to be less difficult to sell than bus bodies and of course, less complicated to manufacture. In fact it is probably true to say that the company would not have prospered as well as it did had it been totally reliant in selling bus bodies, particularly as some of the buses were sold "in house". With the take-over of the sister bus company in 1930, and Bristol Tramway's desire that this local company should standardize its fleet, with replacement buses being supplied by the parent company, the coach building enterprise needed to search for new outlets.

During the era of the sister bus company, William Bence took into his employment during September 1922, a Clifford G. Harding, to manage the bus receipt office, which was actually situated in Mr. Bence's private home. Cliff Harding was a diligent and hard working employee, and was known to turn his hand to any job which was required, including helping out with the service when there were staff shortages in the running crew.

The enthusiasm which so often emanates from the creation of a new business was quite infectious, to the extent that no one gave much thought to the number of hours they worked, and it was not unknown for some staff, including Cliff Harding, to work from 7am to 11pm. In due course Cliff Harding progressed to being in charge of the general office, the post he held when the bus company was taken-over by the Bristol Tramway & Carriage Co. The need to have a local general office and manager, was not part of the BTCC's thinking and, not wishing to lose a loyal and hardworking employee, William invited Harding to transfer his skills and ability to the body building side of the business. Within four years, William was so impressed by Cliff's ability and organisation, that Mr.Clifford Harding was invited onto the Board of Directors in 1934.

With the loss of the bus building contracts, it is not surprising to see that during the first half of the 1930's W.J.Bence Ltd., was producing a large number of goods vehicle bodies, and a smaller quantity of passenger models. However as far as the latter is concerned, Bence had a very loyal and faithful customer in S.G.Wiltshire of Staple Hill, who continued to purchase coaches of the Albion/Bence pedigree throughout most of this decade. Despite the doubts for the future that had existed during the last year or so of the 1920's, as the following decade progressed, the bus body business began to stabilize, then grow, and then improve. William Bence would almost certainly have detected the growth that was occurring in his business, but sadly he did not live to see the end result. At the time of his death he had, for the previous four or five years, been struggling with a breakdown in the relationship with his sons, particularly Henry. The cause of the breakdown and why it occurred was never made public, but no doubt it was over power and direction, subjects which many father and son relationships, especially business relationships have difficulty in coming to terms with. What is known is that William in his Will, left his share capital in the family company to his non directorial granddaughters, and it would appear that this act prompted Harry into creating a partnership with a bankrupt coachbuilder by the name of Willy Jones, paying off Mr.Jones' debts, and forming the coach building company JONES 8 BENCE of Kingswood.

With bus and in particular, coach bodies becoming more luxurious and complex to construct, the number of coach bodies built at Longwell Green was never great, and from available records it would seem that only one was constructed during 1935, rising to seven during 1939 but, understandably, fell away during the following years.

The damage to Bristol's "Home Front" came with quite a vengeance in 1940, with enemy action completely destroying the premises of' Morrish & Sons, an old established firm of coachbuilders. With the constrictions placed upon re-building damaged properties, it was considered by the proprietors of Morrish & Sons, that it was not worth trying to re-establish their business in new premises and accordingly, talks were held between Mr.A.E.Morrish and the man now in total charge of W.J.Bence, Clifford Harding. These talks resulted in Morrish and Harding jointly purchasing the family interest in W.J.Bence & Sons and, in conjunction with Alan S.Aitken, they re-formed the company under the trading style Bence Motor Bodies Ltd. All three became directors of the company and, under their guidance, the company grew in size and subsequently became big enough to take on the big boys of the industry.

As far as can be determined, the majority of the work carried out at Longwell Green during 1940 was the conversion of cars to ambulances, and possibly the building of new fire engines and ambulance bodies. However during the following year, Bristol Tramway & Carriage Co., obtained permission to have a replacement body fitted to one of their old Bristol B-type chassis, and the work was given to the new company. Obviously BTCC was very pleased with the work carried out as this was the start of a good relationship between both companies which was to last for the next thirty-

With Spot left in charge, Mr Bence has lined his buses up along the main road at Stonehill with, nearest to the camera a Reo DD61016 followed by a Daimler AD6631; and three Napiers Registrations AD6105, DD3407 & DD2871. Beyond, the majority of the buses on show are Ford model 'Ts' c1925.

One of Bence's drivers standing behind his charge ready for another days work
c1930.

Bence Motor Services drivers, conductors and an engineer, pose for the camera outside of the Hanham depot in front of one of the company's Napiers single deck buses around 1927.

years. With new buses just not available during the war years, and with some service buses being damaged by enemy action, there had to be a policy of 'patch and mend'. In addition a number of the larger coachbuilders were involved in war-work, and the combination of these facts meant that BTCC's own bodywork shop was extremely busy. This enabled Bence Motor Bodies to carry out a considerable amount of work for BTCC and one or two smaller independent carriers, and it is believed that around 33/34 bodies were produced for BTCC on Bristol B-type chassis during the years 1942-44, some of which went to Bristol Tramways, and some to its sister company Bath Tramways. A number of these bodies had the high capacity passenger carrying arrangement developed during the war years of perimeter seating, which enabled many more standing passengers to be carried than would normally be the case if the conventional seating arrangement had been employed.

During 1944, as the war began to reach its anticipated final conclusion, the state of the public service vehicles operated by the country's bus companies, particularly the body of the bus, was in a dreadful and sometimes dangerous condition, having suffered quite badly from the lack of any proper maintenance, and the over use of the vehicle. Having for five long years been forced to operate a 'patch and make-do' system, the bus companies looked to the Government to see if help could be given to ease the ridged wartime restrictions of what materials could or could not be used by the bodybuilders. Eventually, having succumbed to considerable pressure from both the coach body builders and the bus operators, the Government reacted by authorizing certain of the former to become official repairers of public service vehicle bodies, with Bence Motor Bodies Ltd., being one of the fortunate few. This certainly was just the fillip that the company needed to be able to move forward with added confidence. With new directors at the helm, and a chance to gain a good reputation throughout the industry, it was decided that now was the time to throw off the vestige of the past by dropping the reference to the Bence name, and to trade under the style, LONGWELL GREEN COACHWORKS LTD.

Being situated where it was, the company was in an ideal position to attack the potentially large South Wales market, particularly as that area was at that time, devoid of any coach building industry of its own. One of the companies *LGC* successfully targeted was Rhondda Transport, and its associated company, Devon General. At first, five vehicles were repaired during 1944 for the South Wales Company, including for the very first time at Longwell Green, work on a double deck body. This work for Rhondda Transport gave *LGC* the opportunity of producing bodies of their own design, unlike the work carried out for Bristol Tramways which, as a subsidiary of the Thomas Tilling Group, imposed the standard Tilling design specification on their supplier.

Over the next two or three years, *LGC* carried out a variety of work for a number of customers, both small and large. Understandably, the majority of the work undertaken was in respect of the larger concerns, and during 1947-48. they were required to finish the building of bodies on twenty-one Leyland PDI chassis for

they may, the directors of LGC found themselves unable to secure the same amount of bus body work as they had in the past, with the final order for two double deck bodies on AEC Regent V chassis being secured from a new customer, Pontypridd UDC, in 1965. As it turned out this order was very unique as it was the first and only one ever received for front entrance double deck bodies to be built at Longwell Green.

Although the company tended to specialize in the building of vehicle bodies, there was another aspect of their work, which over the post-war years gradually gained in importance. The work consisted of rebuilding and conversion and, again, Rhondda Transport was a significant customer, starting in 1946 with the rebuilding of a single deck bus and converting it into a tipping lorry. Over the following years, numerous older vehicles were despatched from South Wales to Longwell Green, and given a new lease of life with a body rebuild and fresh livery. Similar work was also undertaken for other Welsh bus companies, as well as for Bristol Tramways, but probably the biggest single customer was Devon General who, in addition to the normal work, had six older double deck buses converted to open top for use on seaside duties around the Torbay area.

The end of this kind of rebuilding/conversion work came around 1959, although the company still continued to rebuild buses which had been involved in accidents for a further six years or so, but all bus and coach body building came to a complete halt in 1966. From then on, the only bodywork carried out was in respect of commercial vehicles, mainly for the nationalized industries operated by British Road Services, and by British Rail.

As previously highlighted, *LGC* began to specialize in the use of fibreglass and their early move into the construction of bus shelters proved to be a reasonable success. Accordingly, as the bus bodywork was coming to an end, so the construction of bus shelters increased, and soon towns as far apart as Cardiff in South Wales and Sheffield in Yorkshire had bus shelters built in Longwell Green. During the mid sixties, the company developed a translucent roof panel and one of Cardiff Corporation's double deck buses, which had been damaged in a low bridge accident, became the first bus to be fitted with a complete roof of these panels. The experiment proved a success, and within a few years a translucent panel in the centre of the roof of double deck buses became a common feature. Such was the success, a new company Longwell Green Plastics was formed for the sole purpose of manufacturing the GRP mouldings and, within a short space of time, had acquired the nearby Warmley Coachworks business.

Sometime in the late 1970's, a new Longwell Green company was formed, with the single intent of acquiring the assets of the old firm and restructuring the company's finances and, although sterling efforts were made to keep the company viable, the directors found themselves "swimming against the tide" of progress. Try as they might, the directors could not save the company and in July 1983 the company went

The output of National-Benzole liveried lorries, built for Colston Fry, are displayed along the main road, with Mr. Fry, standing in front of DD2228. c1924.

The inside of the body shop, showing a number of vehicles under contruction during the late 1950's. Reproduced by kind permission of David G. Elliott.

Sometime around 1950, Bristol Tramways Leyland PDI, KHY400 attempted to get under a low bridge which resulted in the upper deck being badly damaged as shown above. After being returned to Longwell Green the body was rebuilt and C4031 resumed normal duties. Both pictures from the Peter Davey, Bristol Omnibus Photograph Collection.

Two further examples of the body building skills of Longwell Green Coachworks, with above another of the Leyland PDI's C4025 (KHY 394) crossing Durdham Downs, on the No.2 Sea Mills route 26 May 1954. Below is the picture of an older vehicle which had seen a great deal of service during the war years, and which was re-bodied at Longwell Green around 1946. No.2013 (HY 8256) is seen outside of Bristol Zoo in April 1947. Both pictures from the Peter Davey Bristol Omnibus Photograph Collection.

into liquidation after ninety-two years of continuous trading. From a starting point of an idea in the heart of a local skilled man, the business went on to manufacture and produce over 400 bus and/or coach bodies whilst keeping many local people employed: William Bence would surely have every right to be a proud man.

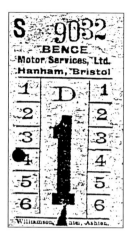
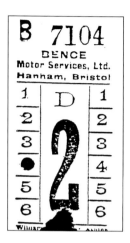

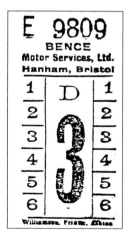
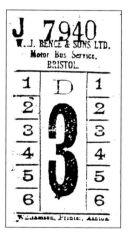

Sample tickets c1930